Kevin Ray

THE IVP NEW TESTAMENT COMMENTARY SERIES

1 Peter

I. Howard Marshall

Grant R. Osborne
series editor

D. Stuart Briscoe
Haddon Robinson
consulting editors

INTERVARSITY PRESS
DOWNERS GROVE, ILLINOIS, USA
LEICESTER, ENGLAND

InterVarsity Press, USA
P.O. Box 1400, Downers Grove, IL 60515-1426, USA
World Wide Web: www.ivpress.com
E-mail: mail@ivpress.com

Inter-Varsity Press, England
38 De Montfort Street, Leicester LE1 7GP, England
World Wide Web: www.ivpbooks.com
E-mail: ivp@uccf.org.uk

InterVarsity Press®, U.S.A., is the book-publishing division of InterVarsity Christian Fellowship/ USA®, a student movement active on campus at hundreds of universities, colleges and schools of nursing in the United States of America, and a member movement of the International Fellowship of Evangelical Students. For information about local and regional activities, write Public Relations Dept., InterVarsity Christian Fellowship/USA, 6400 Schroeder Rd., P.O. Box 7895, Madison, WI 53707-7895, or visit the IVCF website at <www.intervarsity.org>.

Inter-Varsity Press, England, is the publishing division of the Universities and Colleges Christian Fellowship (formerly the Inter-Varsity Fellowship), a student movement linking Christian Unions in universities and colleges throughout Great Britain, and a member movement of the International Fellowship of Evangelical Students. For information about local and national activities write to UCCF, 38 De Montfort Street, Leicester LE1 7GP, email us at email@uccf.org.uk, or visit the UCCF website at www.uccf.org.uk.

USA ISBN 0-8308-1817-0
UK ISBN 0-8511-670-1

Printed in the United States of America ∞

Library of Congress Cataloging-in-Publication Data

Marshall, I. Howard
 1 Peter / I. Howard Marshall.
   p. cm.—(The IVP New Testament commentary series)
  Includes bibliographical references.
  ISBN 0-8308-1817-0
  1. Bible. N.T. Peter, 1st—Commentaries. I. Title. II. Title:
First Peter. III. Series.
 BS2795.3.M37   1990
227'.9207—dc20   *90-41306*
                                                                                            CIP

British Library Cataloguing in Publication Data

Marshall, I. Howard (Ian Howard) 1934-
 1 Peter.
 1. Christianity. Scriptures
 I. Title
 227.92

 ISBN 0-85111-670-1

P	22	21	20	19	18	17	16	15	14	13	12	11	10	9	8	7
Y	19	18	17	16	15	14	13	12	11	10	09	08	07	06	05	

To Haydn and Alex Wainwright
Shepherds of God's Flock

General Preface

In an age of proliferating commentary series, one might easily ask why add yet another to the seeming glut. The simplest answer is that no other series has yet achieved what we had in mind—a series to and from the church, that seeks to move from the text to its contemporary relevance and application.

No other series offers the unique combination of solid, biblical exposition and helpful explanatory notes in the same user-friendly format. No other series has tapped the unique blend of scholars and pastors who share both a passion for faithful exegesis and a deep concern for the church. Based on the New International Version of the Bible, one of the most widely used modern translations, The IVP New Testament Commentary Series builds on the NIV's reputation for clarity and accuracy. Individual commentators indicate clearly whenever they depart from the standard translation as required by their understanding of the original Greek text.

The series contributors represent a wide range of theological traditions, united by a common commitment to the authority of Scripture for Christian faith and practice. Their efforts here are directed toward applying the unchanging message of the New Testament to the ever-changing world in which we live.

Readers will find in each volume, not only traditional discussions of authorship and backgrounds, but useful summaries of principal themes and approaches to contemporary application. To bridge the gap between commentaries that stress the flow of an author's argument but skip over exegetical nettles and those that simply jump from one difficulty to another, we have developed our unique format that expounds the text in uninterrupted form on the upper portion of each page while dealing with other issues underneath in verse-keyed notes. To avoid clutter we have also adopted a social studies note system that keys references to the bibliography.

We offer the series in hope that pastors, students, Bible teachers and small group leaders of all sorts will find it a valuable aid—one that stretches the mind and moves the heart to ever-growing faithfulness and obedience to our Lord Jesus Christ.

Preface

I cannot remember when I first became enamored of 1 Peter, but certainly it sprang to life for me as we read it together in morning Bible studies at the Church of Scotland Seaside Missions in North Berwick in 1951 and 1952. At that time too I became aware of the superb commentary by E. G. Selwyn, which constitutes a landmark in the study of the epistle. (One could almost say that the student who reads Selwyn has no need to look at any earlier commentaries.) Later I studied 1 Peter more academically as a set text in the University of Aberdeen B.D. degree. But I cannot forget that my earliest serious study of it was in the living context of a group engaged in mission, and I am grateful for the incentive posed by this series of commentaries to combine an academic and a practical approach to the letter.

Although this commentary aims to give a good exegetical foundation for understanding the message of 1 Peter, it will not render the use of other commentaries superfluous. Selwyn's work (using the Greek text) is too full and technical for general use. The same is true of the commentary by F. W. Beare. The major scholarly work in recent times is the

German commentary by L. Goppelt; it is worthy to be placed alongside Selwyn. The works of J. N. D. Kelly and E. Best are among the most useful helps for the student, and the former of these, being fuller in its discussions, is highly recommended. On a smaller scale the commentary by C. E. B. Cranfield is outstanding, not only for its scholarly exegesis but also for its exposition of the letter as the Word of God for today.

In the period between the original writing of the present work and its publication, no less than four important works have appeared. I have been grateful for the opportunity to revise my material in the light of them. The general reader is well served with the concise new volume in the Tyndale New Testament Commentary series by W. Grudem (with an important discussion of 3:19-21), and the specialist will find much in the lengthy and learned Word Biblical Commentary on the Greek text by J. R. Michaels. In addition there is a scholarly practical exposition of *The Message of 1 Peter* by E. P. Clowney in the The Bible Speaks Today series, and the significant technical study on *Hermeneutic and Composition in 1 Peter* by W. L. Schutter. With their varying conclusions on different points these works reflect how the study of 1 Peter continues to pose problems for scholars to resolve.

Many existing commentaries tend to ignore the vital question: What has 1 Peter to say to us today? I have deliberately kept this question in mind at every point in order to allow the challenging teaching of 1 Peter to speak afresh. The case could be made that if one were to be shipwrecked on a desert island and allowed to have only one of the New Testament letters as a companion, then 1 Peter would be the ideal choice, so rich is its teaching, so warm its spirit, and so comforting its message in a hostile environment.

I. Howard Marshall

General Introduction

SPIRITUAL HEALTH WARNING:
ATTENDING THIS EVENT CAN
SERIOUSLY AFFECT YOUR FUTURE!

So ran the wording at the foot of a notice inviting people to a meeting about a project entitled "Dirty Hands," which was concerned to involve Christians in meeting the needs of the world around them. It could indeed be dangerous to attend the meeting: Some Christians would find themselves being challenged to spend time doing relief work in Ethiopia or Bangladesh and actually responding to the challenge!

Do you expect to be affected in the same way by reading a book? All of us expect this with some books. If I read a book on how to be a better do-it-yourself person, I do indeed hope that it will change me to the extent that I can cope with household repairs more efficiently. There is not much point in reading the book otherwise! But with other books we brace ourselves to be cool and critical so that we are not influenced in ways that we do not want to be influenced.

Peter's first letter was written to change people, and it still has that power today. So if you do not want to see your Christian life being affected, maybe you should stop right now and get your money back. I have no doubt, however, that many of its first readers read it in the same spirit as I tackled my do-it-yourself book. They wanted to be changed. They wanted to find the answers to some of their problems.

If one thing stands out clearly from this letter, it is that Christian congregations were already beginning to know what it was like to live in a hostile environment where other people made it tough for them just because they were Christians. They needed help to cope positively with that situation, and this letter was written to meet their need.

The congregations in question lived in the area that we now know as Turkey but which at that time was composed of several administrative areas of the Roman Empire. From other information of a later date we know that this general area was perhaps more prone to attacks on Christians than others. The book of Revelation, written later in the first century, offers ample testimony to the rise of official persecution of Christians by the state. And Pliny, the Roman governor of Bithynia early in the second century, found himself having to tackle the problem of prosecutions brought against people who were Christians.

But even at this stage it seems that state action was rare (Pliny acted only when prosecutions were brought that he could not overlook) and that what Christians had to fear was more in the nature of social ostracism, unfriendly acts by neighbors, pressure on Christian wives from pagan husbands, masters taking it out on Christian slaves and other actions of that kind. It was sufficient, in any case, to make life uncomfortable. And it was known that Christians elsewhere had suffered imprisonment and even death for their faith. Jesus himself was executed on a Roman "gallows" like a slave, and he had warned his followers not to expect any better treatment.

From the letter we can tell that its recipients were a mixed group of people. The fact that slaves are addressed, but not their masters, may suggest that there weren't many Christian masters in the congregations. Likewise, the nature of the instructions given to wives in comparison with those given to husbands may suggest that there were more Christian wives than Christian husbands in mixed marriages. The readers appear to have been mainly converts from pagan religions rather than Jews, but they were probably a mixture of both. Their congregations were led by elders, but, if Peter has judged his audience correctly, they probably included quite a number of new converts.

As for the author himself, he is Peter, the original leader of the twelve apostles and yet a person about whom we know remarkably little in comparison with Paul. We do know that he was writing about the kind of situation which he had personally experienced and that, before long, he would pay the supreme price for being a Christian at the hands of the Emperor Nero. So, although he is writing to congregations whom he probably did not know personally, he knew their situation and wrote to them accordingly.

What did he have to say to them? He writes a letter that follows the conventions of contemporary letter-writing: opening and closing greetings bracketing the main body (1:1-2; 1:3—5:11; 5:12-14). It is exactly the same form as we find in Paul, whose letters seem to have set the pattern for other Christians. Like Paul, Peter begins with thanksgiving to God that is couched in general terms (as in Ephesians) rather than referring specifically to the congregations and that expresses the essence of a gospel of hope despite the gathering clouds. Various themes that are developed later come in these opening verses (1:3-12). The rest of the letter falls into three main parts.

First, Peter states the basic characteristics of the Christian life; he gives fundamental teaching on what it means to be a Christian as well as its practical implications (1:13—2:10).

Second, building on this theological foundation, Peter discusses how Christians should conduct themselves in various relationships of social and family life. Already in this section the problem of relationships with people who are not Christians begins to surface (2:11—3:12).

But it is in the remainder of the letter that Peter directly addresses the possibility of persecution and opposition (3:13—5:11). Here he encourages his readers to give a courageous witness for Christ, remembering how Christ himself bore testimony to the powers of evil. Peter discusses the Christians' new way of life and the need for strong congregational life to give them inner strength. Then he shows how persecution is a cause for joy and, at the same time, a means of testing the church. He also gives further teaching on the need for good leadership in the church.

The reader of the letter soon becomes aware that much of this teaching is relevant to all Christians and not just to those experiencing hostility and persecution. As some scholars have pointed out, the letter is concerned as much, if not more, with Christian action in the world as with Christian suffering. The emphasis lies on persevering in doing good, and active evangelism is assumed. Therefore, although the letter does say much about hostility toward Christians and their suffering, this forms the framework for Peter's teaching rather than being its unique theme.

Consequently, it would not be difficult, for example, to use this letter as a manual for a class in church membership or as preparation for baptism or confirmation. Some gaps would remain in the topics discussed, but they would not be many. Guided by this impression, a number of scholars have argued that this document is not so much a letter to persecuted Christians as the report of a sermon (or even more than one sermon) for a baptismal service, giving teaching for new converts. This interpretation of the document is not satisfactory for various reasons, but it contains an important element of truth: Teaching given repeatedly to young Christians lies at the root of the letter. Much of the teaching is not directly and explicitly on persecution; it is basic instruction for young (and old) Christians that remains relevant in the special situation of hostility.

This shows that, although it was written to a specific situation, 1 Peter had a message for all Christians in the first century. As a result, we can without too much difficulty loosen it from its first-century setting and read it as a message for Christians today.

Because this series of commentaries aims to read the New Testament in such a manner as to hear its contemporary message, let me state briefly the approach that I have adopted here. I have assumed that any book of the New Testament was written to convey the author's message to a particular set of readers. The author was not writing for us, although no doubt he was aware that much of what he said was applicable to a more general audience than, say, Christians in Asia Minor. Consequently, we have to ask the question in the form: If this was the author's message to his original readers, how does that message apply to us who live in different cultures and specific situations from them? We have to find out first, what the author was saying to the original readers, and second, how what he was saying to them applies to us.

The first task is known as *exegesis*, the stock-in-trade of the typical scholarly commentary on the New Testament. It uses all the accepted tools of biblical scholarship summed up as the grammatico-historical method. Its aim is to explain what the author was saying by putting his writing in its historical, social, cultural and theological context, and also, as an essential part of this process, to clarify things said in the text that were readily understandable to the original readers but that are no longer intelligible to modern readers (such as the meaning of the word *redeemed* in 1:18).

The second process is what is known as *exposition*, or *application*, and here the rules of the game are less clearly defined. Should women today not wear *gold jewelery and fine clothes* just because Peter says they shouldn't (3:3)? Are Christians to regard themselves as *aliens and strangers in the world* because that is how Peter describes them (2:11)? Can we go on living as though the Second Coming of Jesus was very near (1:5-7; 5:4), although nineteen hundred years of church history suggest that a different perspective is needed? Are we to believe in the existence of a personal devil (5:8) or indeed in the existence of a personal Holy Spirit (1:11)?

In attempting to answer these questions two principles should be followed. The first is to recognize that various parts of what any biblical writer wrote may have been meant specifically for readers in a given situation. In every case we have to ask what basic, universally valid biblical principles come to expression in the specific teaching, and then apply these principles to ourselves. For example, we may not be under threat of physical violence for being Christians like some of Peter's readers. In such a case the specific teaching may not be directly applicable to us; nevertheless, we can still read it and find that the underlying principles may be of more general application to us.

The second principle is to recognize differences between our situation and that of the original readers and reapply the original teaching in ways that take account of these differences. Certainly a great deal of biblical teaching applies directly to us without much need for reapplication because we are sinful men and women just like the people of the first century. But in places the situations are different. For example, slavery does not exist today. But, as we shall see, the teaching given by Peter to slaves (2:18-20) arises out of a general principle about fulfilling the obligations imposed by a particular relationship and can then be reformulated to apply to different situations from that of slavery.

In contrast, we may find ourselves facing problems and situations that were unknown in the ancient world. For example, the existence of nuclear weapons may constitute such a difference in the means of waging war as to make us ask whether the morality of war is different for present-day Christians from what it was in biblical times. When this happens, we clearly have to gain principles from the Bible (not necessarily drawn from passages on warfare but more widely) that can be reapplied to our situation.

To follow this method is, of course, to assume that the New Testament is the expression of eternally valid principles, or, put otherwise, that it is the written Word of God whose authority we accept. To justify this assumption would go beyond the scope of this introduction.

Special Introduction

In the general introductory comments on 1 Peter a number of points have been made and a number of issues omitted which require fuller comment and some scholarly justification. For a helpful survey of recent scholarship, see the essays gathered together in C. Perrot (1980), especially the survey by E. Cothenet (pp. 13-42), and also R. P. Martin (1986).

Genre and Sources As indicated above, 1 Peter has the formal characteristics of a letter. But is this impression more than superficial? Has material of a different kind been put into letter form? As the document stands, it lacks personal material —no hint of personal contacts between the writer and recipients such as we find in Paul's letters. This may indicate that the writer did not know his readers and their situation in any detail. But we should remember that many letters show these characteristics, and there is nothing surprising about a Christian leader writing to Christians with whom he had no direct contact but whom he nevertheless knew to be in need of teaching and encouragement. The document undoubtedly is conceived by its author as a letter and should be read as such.

Some commentators have discussed at length the kind of material that went into the letter and shown that it contains various types of Christian teaching. A discussion of this issue in detail would be inappropriate in the present volume since it makes little difference in understanding the actual text of 1 Peter—as opposed to using the letter as evidence for the history of the early church.

Suffice it to say: Theories which confidently identify the major part of the letter as a baptismal sermon or as a combination of a baptismal liturgy and a sermon (1:3—4:11; 4:12—5:11) have rightly not gained support. What we see is the free and creative use of material from different teaching situations in the early church.

A certain amount of the teaching finds its ultimate source in the *tradition of the sayings of Jesus.* Note especially 1:4 (Lk 12:33); 1:13 (Lk 12:35); 1:18 (Mk 10:45) and 3:14 (Mt 5:10). Scholars disagree considerably as to whether this teaching came to the author of the letter directly, as the memories of an eyewitness, or indirectly, via the traditions that eventually found written form in the Gospels (Maier 1985).

Another important inspiration is *the use of the Old Testament.* Few New Testament books show so rich and varied a use of Old Testament teaching, both in quotation and in allusion (see Schlosser's essay in Perrot [1980:65-96] and especially Schutter [1989]).

A third source of material is *the common teaching of the early church.* First Peter is in no sense "out on a limb" in its teaching or vocabulary in the way that is true of, say, Hebrews and 1 John with their quite distinctive worlds of ideas. Its theology closely reflects the primitive *kerygma* (doctrinal statements of the gospel) and *paraenesis* (ethical teaching arising out of the gospel) as these can be reconstructed from the evidence of the New Testament generally. The thought is closer to that of Paul than of any other New Testament writer, and the similarities go deeper than those due simply to the use of common Christian ideas. The concepts of being "in Christ" and "union with Christ in his death" are indicative of this.

These three basic sources affected the materials used by Peter. Specifically we may refer to the following types or "forms" of material:

1. Teaching material formulated in connection with the instruction of new converts.

2. Teaching material to instruct in Christian ethics. The close similarities with other letters demonstrate the common use of "household codes."

3. Teaching specifically related to persecution. Although Selwyn's "persecution document" has not won a lot of support, the case for a common pattern of teaching about how to face persecution seems to me to be adequately established (Selwyn 1947:439-58).

4. So-called hymns—short compositions presenting the person and work of Christ. Their careful wording suggests that they were intended to be memorized and perhaps recited or sung. The existence of such hymns as source material for 1 Peter (in particular, 1:3-5; 2:22-25; 3:18-22 and 5:5-9) is a matter of controversy. Whatever the situation is, I think it is worth observing that here, as elsewhere in the New Testament, Peter is probably not quoting lengthy pieces of formulated tradition word for word with little change. My impression is that he uses a good deal of existing vocabulary, phraseology and thinking which permits us to infer the existence of patterns of teaching that he uses without being slavishly bound by them. That is to say, Peter is an author, making his own fresh use of the common teaching of the church rather than simply repeating what others had previously said.

Authorship The author of the letter identifies himself as the apostle Peter. Scholarship is strongly divided on whether or not the letter is pseudonymous:

Authentic—Bénétreau, Clowney, Cranfield, Grudem, Hunter, Michaels (with some hesitation), Neugebauer, Schelkle, Selwyn, Spicq, Stibbs and Walls

Inauthentic—Beare, Best, Brox, Goppelt, Schutter

Undecided—Kelly

German scholarship in particular seems to assume that the debate has been settled in favor of pseudonymity. The current tendency to see pseudonymity at work wherever possible has enveloped 1 Peter (so that the only New Testament writings which can be attributed to their named authors are some seven letters of Paul, all the rest being pseudonymous or anonymous). But, if ever there was a weak case for pseudonymity, surely it is in respect to this letter. The arguments briefly are as follows

(Goppelt 1978:66-70):

1. The good command of Greek and the use of the Septuagint are unlikely for an ignorant Galilean fisherman. The alleged difficulty is not simply that the letter is written in Greek but that it is written in a somewhat cultured style.

2. A lack of known links exists between Peter and Christians in Asia Minor. Why should he write to them? And why should he write to an area evangelized by Paul without even mentioning him?

3. The worldwide persecution reflected in the letter arose after Peter's death, either in the late first century or even in the time of Trajan (A.D. 98—117). The description of the persecuting power of Rome as "Babylon" is said to have been first developed by the Jews after A.D. 70.

4. The letter shows no concrete characteristics of Peter, such as eyewitness recollections of Jesus. The reminiscences of the sayings of Jesus rest on the church's tradition rather than on personal memory.

5. The letter shows a religious idiom that developed against the background of Hellenistic Judaism rather than Palestinian Judaism.

Thirty years ago, in his brilliant introduction to the exposition by Alan Stibbs, my colleague Andrew Walls refuted this case. More recently J. A. T. Robinson (1976:140-69) has again tackled the issue in the context of a discussion of the dating of the letter. I doubt whether anything more needs to be said. Nevertheless, we must briefly respond to the points just listed:

1. It is probably difficult for many of us in the English-speaking world to appreciate the degree to which bilingualism can flourish in other communities. When a ship is lost off Greenland, the coast guards can give their report in perfect English on a radio news program, while most of us have to think twice as to what their native language is, never mind replying to them in it. Why should we underestimate the culture of a member of a middle-class Galilean fishing family? The extent of the good Greek in 1 Peter can be greatly exaggerated, as has been shown by Nigel Turner, who argues that a Semitic style of Greek has been given a superficial and incomplete veneer of good style and that this could be the work of an amanuensis (1976:121-31). It is possible, despite Wayne Grudem's objections (1988:23-24), that the letter was written "through Silvanus" (about whose competence in Greek we admittedly know noth-

ing at all). Where is the hard evidence to prove that neither Peter nor Silvanus could have written the Greek of this letter?

2. It is puzzling why Peter writes to distant communities in the heart of Asia Minor. (The possibility that he evangelized in this area cannot be ruled out, but the letter itself does not suggest this.) Yet we can easily hypothesize that visitors to Rome from the area told Peter of the situation of the church and that he wrote this letter for their benefit. The lack of reference to Paul is not something to worry about. The area from which the readers came was largely not evangelized by Paul, and if he was not with Peter at the time the letter was written, there was no need to mention him. Perhaps more surprising is that Peter writes to communities of mainly Gentile Christians when he was "the apostle to the circumcision." But we may question how long the division of labor in Galatians 2:7 could have continued. It was, after all, Peter who evangelized the pagan household of Cornelius.

3. It is false to claim that the letter reflects "worldwide" persecution. The evidence from the letter points to widespread hostile reactions to Christians but not to organized, state-inspired persecution. The attitudes reflect a period before the rise of state persecution. As for the designation of Rome as "Babylon," this was current well before A.D. 70, as C. P. Thiede (1987) has shown.

4. We know far too little of Peter to be able to say what he could and could not have written. In fact, occasional hints in the letter make better sense if they reflect his personal experiences and knowledge of Jesus. He is no different from all the other letter writers in the New Testament in making no direct reference to the contents of the Gospels and mentioning the teaching of Jesus more allusively.

5. The influence of Hellenistic Judaism on Peter cannot be excluded. After the incidents in Acts 12 and 15 he no longer remained in Jerusalem but traveled more widely. Moreover, he was part of a church that consisted of Aramaic-speaking and Greek-speaking Jewish Christians. There is not the slightest reason why he should not have been influenced by Hellenistic Judaism. When will scholars stop making rigid divisions between Palestinian and Hellenistic Jewish Christians?

None of the arguments for pseudonymity, therefore, is adequate to refute the impression made by the letter itself. We may also point out positively that the letter totally lacks the signs of later composition: no reference to the danger of heresies such as incipient Gnosticism, no characterization of the state as a malevolent beast, no trace of the posthumous honoring of Peter, and none of the developed apparatus of pseudonymity. The letter's theology and church organization are not developed in the direction of early Catholicism.

The Situation of the Readers   The hostility faced by the letter's recipients is perhaps the element that stands out most to contemporary readers. Its presence obviously cannot be denied. Yet we can ask whether this is the major constitutive factor affecting the composition of the letter.

J. H. Elliott (1981) has adopted a sociological approach to the letter. He argues that Christians are seen as "resident aliens" in society, a distinct class who suffered from the accompanying tensions of not belonging in the world and who therefore needed the security of belonging to a heavenly home. This explains the strong use of house imagery in the letter. The readers were a "conversionist" sect faced with external threats and the consequent danger to their own inner cohesiveness. In light of this, the writer needed to: (1) reassert their distinctive communal identity, (2) reinforce their group cohesion, and (3) plausibly explain the compatibility of their experience and their expectations on both the social and spiritual level. Although Elliott's book contains much useful information about the first-century situation, he pushes his case too far and makes too much of the concept of "house" and the need for cohesiveness in the church (see the criticisms by Bénétreau 1984:67-68).

A much more plausible reading of the letter is given by L. Goppelt (1982: 161-78 summarizes his position). He stresses the situation of the readers as people who were discriminated against rather than being actually persecuted. The discrimination arose out of the unwillingness of Christians to take part in societal life associated with idolatry. The theme of the letter is not persecution as such but rather the situation of Christians in society and their consequent responsibilities. This accents the good behavior that they should practice and maintain despite malicious attacks.

Essentially the same position was developed independently by

F. Neugebauer (1979), who argues that the letter is concerned with the positive behavior of Christians in society. He draws attention to the stress on doing good, from which Christians must not be diverted by their hostile experiences. The letter is, therefore, not an incentive to martyrdom; Peter does not glorify suffering. His point is not that Christians should endure to death but that they should persist in doing good.

Possibly Goppelt and Neugebauer have been too much influenced by a contemporary stress on the need for Christians to exercise social witness in the world by a Christian presence instead of withdrawing from the world and its concerns. Alternatively, we might argue that the present situation of the church has enabled them to develop a better insight into the teaching of Peter. What must not be overlooked in this stress on Christian living in the world is that, for Peter, the world is a place where Christians are liable to suffer. The number of uses of *suffer* and *suffering* in this letter is out of all proportion to its size (2:19 note). There are many places in the world where contemporary readers of 1 Peter live in circumstances much more like that of the original readers than is the case for Christians in North America and Europe. First Peter is primarily meant for them. We are those who overhear the message and find how much it has to say to us—not only to arm and prepare us *if [we] should suffer for doing what is right* but also to give us the true perspective on the world when we fail to recognize the *roaring lion looking for someone to devour.*

The Theology of the Letter We know so little about the theology of Peter from other sources that we are almost totally dependent on this letter for our understanding of his thought. What we have here is certainly compatible with what we find elsewhere in the speeches ascribed to Peter in Acts (Selwyn 1947:33-6). The letter itself reflects a rich theology that shares much in common with what we know of the thinking of the earliest church, but it also contains its own personal characteristics and is contextualized (to use current jargon) to meet the needs of the readers.

Note briefly these varied aspects of Peter's thinking:

1. It is centered on God the Father and Jesus Christ (who is implicitly his Son, 1:3). The allusion to God the Father, Jesus Christ and the Spirit in close conjunction with one another in 1:2 is similar to other statements in the New Testament that have a trinitarian flavor. As Father, God

is characterized by loving concern for his children; yet he is still the impartial judge, who is to be revered and honored by his people.

There is no sense in which Christ replaces God at the center of the Christian's consciousness. Christ himself is probably regarded as pre-existent, although Peter does not stress this for its own sake (1:20). He describes Jesus' demeanor during his passion in terms of the Suffering Servant of Yahweh and emphasizes that he *suffered.* Jesus' death is seen as a redemptive sacrifice, but it is closely linked with his resurrection (and in connection with the latter Peter develops his unique understanding of the visit of Christ to the spirits in prison to proclaim his victory over them). Lastly, Christ's return in glory is the object of eager anticipation by his disciples.

2. Christians are sinners who used to live in the darkness of paganism but have been brought into an experience of salvation. They were the object of God's choice, have been born anew by the Word of God and now live by faith. They entered into the people of God by baptism. (The Lord's Supper is not directly mentioned except perhaps for a secondary allusion in 2:3.) In all this their Christian life is especially characterized by hope in the future coming of Jesus. Yet, although Peter tends to write of salvation as a future experience, he emphasizes the reality of the believer's present experience of divine grace and uses the "in Christ" language familiar from Paul.

3. Christians are the people of God and are described in terms drawn from the Old Testament descriptions of Israel. This point has special emphasis because Peter implies that the physical people of Israel, the Jews, are no longer part of spiritual Israel unless they believe in Christ. Here Peter is clearly at one with Paul, and what is said is nothing more than the theological outworking of his experience in Acts 10.

4. The Old Testament is seen as a Christian book—at least in its prophetic teaching about the Messiah and his people. Peter alludes extensively to it and includes an important justification of the Christian use made of it (1:10-12). Early Christian testimonies about Jesus, which identified him as the chosen "stone," are picked up and used. A very complex method of interpreting the biblical material in the letter has been depicted by W. L. Schutter (1989).

5. First Peter has a strong emphasis on Christian conduct: Christians

are to be the holy people of God. At the same time, they must live in such a way as to make a good impression on non-Christians. There is an implicit missionary motivation here: Christian conduct is an important ingredient in evangelism (compare 2:12; 3:1, 15-16) alongside the actual preaching of the gospel to non-Christians, which Peter assumes to be taking place as a matter of course. Peter shares with Paul an emphasis on the need to have and obey a conscience that is governed by obedience to God's will. He also thinks of Christians as being united with Christ in his sufferings and in sharing his attitude toward sin. This is close to the Pauline concept of dying and rising with Christ, but Peter expresses it in his own way.

6. The church is especially important for Peter. He is writing to congregations who form living temples of God, whose members share together in teaching and service and who are characterized by deep love and affection for one another. The members must have deep mutual respect, and leaders in particular are to be respected and obeyed.

7. Peter has a developed doctrine of suffering. He sees it in a variety of ways: as something that God allows as a form of judgment or as a trial to prove genuine faith, as a consequence of Satanic opposition to the people of God, as a means of witness to a hostile world and, above all, as a share in the experience of Christ in union with him. Those who suffer can rejoice because of the future hope of glory but also because in the experience itself they experience the grace of God and his power to keep them (see Millauer 1976; Bénétreau 1984:259-63).

8. Peter has a lively sense of the spiritual dimensions of Christian experience. He firmly believes in angels, the devil and other evil powers. Above all, he believes that Christ has already overcome supernatural evil powers and made them subject to himself; ultimately, the evil powers cannot overcome Christians (Reicke 1946; Dalton 1965; France 1977).

9. Finally, we note the prominence of the Holy Spirit in the letter. He is active both in prophesying the coming of Christ and in the preaching of the good news about him (1:11-12). He sanctifies believers and, in the midst of suffering and persecution, he is especially present with them, as Jesus had promised (Mk 13:11). These few headings will indicate something of the scope and richness of the thinking in this letter (Stibbs 1959:178-92).

Outline of 1 Peter

1:1-2 _____**Opening Greeting**

1:3-12 _____**Thanksgiving**

1:13—2:10 ____**The Basic Characteristics of Christian Living**
    1:13-21 _____Hope and Obedience
    1:22—2:3 ____Love and Purity
    2:4-10 _____The Spiritual House and the Chosen People

2:11—3:12 ____**Social Conduct**
    2:11-12 _____Strangers in the World
    2:13-17 _____The Ruling Authorities
    2:18-20 _____Slaves and their Masters
    2:21-25 _____The Basis for Christian Living
    3:1-7 _____Wives and Husbands
    3:8-12 _____General Instructions

3:13—5:11 ____**The Christian Attitude toward Hostility**
    3:13-17 _____The Blessings and Opportunities of the Persecuted
    3:18-22 _____The Significance of Christ's Victory
    4:1-6 _____Maintaining a Christian Lifestyle
    4:7-11 _____The Life of the Christian Congregation
    4:12-19 _____Suffering, Joy and Judgment
    5:1-5 _____Leadership in the Church
    5:6-11 _____Concluding Practical Advice and Encouragement

5:12-14 _____**Closing Greetings**

COMMENTARY

☐ Opening Greeting (1:1-2)

My sister used to receive letters from her friend Bob in the local Youth for Christ group that invariably began in this sort of way: "Dear Margaret, Greetings in the name of our risen and wonderful Lord." The exuberance of the language sometimes caused us a little amusement, but Bob was actually doing just what the first Christians did. They began their letters with a greeting that followed the pattern found in Jewish letters of the time but with a distinctive Christian flavor. The greeting had three basic parts: (1) the naming of the sender, (2) the naming of the recipient or recipients, and (3) an expression of good wishes. In each part the Christian character of the writing was quite obvious, and so it is here.

The Sender (1:1) The first person ever to have the name Peter may well have been Simon, the brother of Andrew and one of the first disciples. Jesus gave him the Aramaic name *Cephas,* which means "rock," but he came to be generally known in the church by the corresponding Greek word *Petros.*

By identifying himself as an apostle, Peter gives his credentials and authority to write a letter which will convey the promises and commands that God has given to him for his people. He has been personally commissioned by Jesus Christ as a missionary, and this carries with it authority to convey his message to the church. Although, therefore, this letter is a human composition, its message ultimately comes from God and is inspired by the Spirit (1:11).

The Recipients (1:1-2) The readers are identified at some length in a way which specifically characterizes them as Christians and sets the tone for the rest of the letter. These Christians lived in the Roman provinces which occupied the area of modern Turkey. They were a set of scattered groups and perhaps isolated individuals in a wide territory. In this respect they resembled the many Jews who lived in small communities scattered throughout the ancient world, and Peter's wording deliberately echoes the self-description of the Jews as the scattered people outside their homeland.

On the one hand, they were God's chosen ("elect") people, in that he had called them and they had responded (2:9). On the other hand, they were separate from their fellow human beings, resident aliens in a foreign land (2:11), committed to a different lifestyle and thought odd by their fellows. Thus their actual way of life in a non-Christian and often hostile world symbolized their citizenship in God's kingdom. Here then at the outset of the letter Peter fastens on the theme he will develop in the letter as a whole—the situation of Christians in an environment to which they do not belong and from which they may well expect an unsympathetic reaction. Christians in the world today may find themselves in a similar situation within some countries, but in others, even though the majority of the population may not be practicing Christians,

---

Notes: **1:1** The ordinary secular form of greeting in a Greek letter is illustrated in Acts 23:26; it is slightly Christianized in Jas 1:1. The Jewish form is accessible in 2 Macc 1:1. Paul echoes a form of it (which was not confined to opening greetings in letters) in Gal 6:16.

The use of *elect* exemplifies the way in which Peter describes his readers in terms used in the Old Testament to describe Israel as the people of God. It is difficult to resist the impression that Peter saw the church as the spiritual heir of Israel. The early church was confronted with the problem that the nation of Israel was the object of God's promises to its physical ancestors, and yet by and large it had rejected the Messiah, Jesus. It seems clear that for the church those who rejected the Messiah ceased to be God's people, although his promises were still offered to them. The theme of God's choice of believers in Jesus as his people reappears in 2:4-10 where it is linked to the thought of Jesus himself as God's chosen agent. God's choice is seen in his *calling* of the readers to a life of holiness and ultimately to a share in his own glory (1:15; 2:9; 3:9; 5:10).

From the time of the exile onwards many Jews lived outside Palestine and formed the Dispersion (or "scattering"; Jn 7:35). On the whole, they retained an intense loyalty to their nation and to its temple as the focal point of their religion. They continued to follow the

they may on the whole be treated with toleration. In both cases they need to remember that they belong to God, steering the difficult path of not living in a worldly manner while at the same time bearing a loving witness in the world.

This basic description of Christians as God's chosen people is developed in a clear trinitarian structure. Three phrases indicate the origin, manner and goal of their election. The effect is to confirm that the readers are truly God's people in a relationship that the hostile world cannot break.

First, their election took place because God the Father *foreknew* them. This does not mean that God chose them because he knew in advance that they would respond to his call, but simply that God took the initiative and chose them before they had done anything to deserve it. Whether this also means that God determined *how* they would respond is a moot point on which theologians disagree. Second, God's acceptance of them was brought about by the Holy Spirit who transferred them out of the sphere of evil into that of God, with all that this implied for their behavior. Right from the beginning of their Christian experience the Spirit was active in their lives to set God's seal on them as his people and to initiate the new way of life that should characterize the children of God.

Third, the purpose of God's act was that they should show obedience inasmuch as they had been consecrated to Jesus Christ. Just as the covenant between God and Israel was sealed by a ritual in which the people

---

Jewish way of life as a community centered on the local synagogue. Christians naturally took over the imagery (see Jas 1:1).

The readers were scattered through five Roman provinces. Pontus and Bithynia (here separated from each other) formed one province. The apparently strange order in the list is best explained on the theory that the messenger bringing the letter from Rome by sea landed at Amisus on the north coast of Asia Minor and did a circular tour of the provinces. A similar journey is attested by Josephus (Ant. 16:21-3).

1:2 *Who have been chosen* is repetition in the NIV of *elect* in verse 1 to secure a smoother sentence.

Foreknowledge is the literal equivalent of Gk *prognosis,* but the Gk word has the sense of choice and love rather than of knowledge (Num 16:5; Amos 3:2).

Through the sanctifying work is literally "in sanctification" and expresses the way in which God's choice and its effects take place. The phrase anticipates the way in which Peter will stress that Christians constitute the people of God who are called to holiness in every aspect of their life (1:15-16, 22; 2:5, 9).

Sprinkling people with blood is an unusual ritual. The background to the idea of a

---

were sprinkled with the blood of a sacrifice (Ex 24:7-8), so Christians can be regarded as dedicated to God by being *sprinkled* with the blood of Jesus. Their acceptance by faith of his death as an atoning sacrifice for them means that they are bound to him and will express this fact by obeying his commands.

The Greeting (1:2) Finally, Peter expresses in writing what he prays for his friends, namely that they will continue to experience in full measure God's gracious favor and the blessings which flow from it. In this brief phrase the whole of Christian doctrine is summed up in terms of the source of our salvation and its actual content. *Grace* sums up the free, unmerited love of God toward his people. *Peace* (3:11; 5:14) is one of the many words used to describe the content of salvation; it conjures up not only the thought of reconciliation with God but also the idea of the positive blessings that he bestows on his people.

□ Thanksgiving (1:3-12)

Many Christians living in the so-called free world would think twice about voluntarily living in a country where they are deprived of religious liberty and face discrimination, abuse and even penalties if they step outside strict laws. The prospect of suffering is one that we do not face willingly. A person who goes to the hospital to face a major operation, with its accompanying pain and inconvenience, often does so with apprehension. It may be helpful to assure the patient that the painful experience will last a comparatively short time and that a full cure can be confidently expected at the end of it all. Fortified by faith in the word of the surgeon the patient can face the trial ahead with hope for the future and even with a certain relief and happiness.

To be a Christian in Peter's time meant facing uncertain and unpleasant experiences from the surrounding world. A person might well hes-

---

covenant sealed with blood, which is expressed in the cup-saying at the Last Supper (1 Cor 11:25), is found in Ex 24:7-8. Further meditation on this passage led to the use of this metaphor here. It is possible that the word *sprinkling* might convey a secondary allusion to baptism, but there is no evidence elsewhere in the New Testament that the water used in baptism as a symbol of the Spirit could also symbolize the blood of Christ; indeed, such a double meaning for the symbol would be rather confusing. Nor is an allusion to the purification of lepers (Lev 14:6-7; Grudem 1988:52-53) likely.

Grace is a favorite word in the letter (1:2, 10, 13; 2:19, 20; 3:7; 4:10; 5:5, 10, 12). It

itate to join a Christian group for fear of the consequences or quietly opt out because the demands were too great. One of Peter's aims in his letter, then, was to encourage his readers by giving them grounds for solid hope in the ultimate future so that they might face the immediate future with equanimity, courage and even joy. Right at the beginning of the letter he sets this mood in what is, so far as its form is concerned, an expression of thanks to God.

Just as the opening greeting of 1 Peter followed a set pattern characteristic of first-century writers, so too the rest of the letter was to some extent governed by conventions. In ordinary letters some kind of expression of good wishes to the recipient frequently followed the greeting. A random example, from a letter written by a traveler to his family back at home, shows this kind of beginning:

> Apion to Epimachus his father and lord many greetings. Before all things I pray that you are in health, and that you prosper and fare well continually together with my sister and her daughter and my brother. I thank the lord Serapis that when I was in peril on the sea he saved me immediately. When I came to Miseni . . . (Kee 1973:264)

Here we see how the writer gives what we could call a "prayer report," telling of how he prays for his family and commenting on how his own prayers had been answered. Many New Testament letters begin like this. A variant on the pattern is direct thanksgiving to God or a statement of why he is to be praised using the form "Blessed be God . . ." Paul uses this pattern in 2 Corinthians 1:3-4 and Ephesians 1:3-4. There then follows a reasoned statement for giving this thanks to God.

Generally in Paul's letters the thanksgiving serves as an introduction to the main body in that it mentions themes which will be taken up later and thus sets the tone for what follows. It looks as though Peter follows the same practice, for the thought of joy and hope in the midst of trial

---

expresses the attitude which a loving God (5:10) shows to his people. He shows grace—that is, favor—to the humble who have no strength of their own and do not struggle for position but simply trust in his goodness (5:5). But the word can also be used to mean the actual expression of God's love as experienced by his people and thus be virtually equivalent to *salvation* (1:10; 3:7; 5:12). It can also in effect mean the sum total of the spiritual gifts that God bestows on the church (4:10) or the special experience of his love that is associated with the second coming of Christ (1:13). For the use in 2:19-20 see the discussion of these verses.

and suffering is dominant in this thanksgiving. But Peter is so full of ideas at this point that he produced a complicated set of reasons for praising God. It is not easy to trace a clear line of thought. People who "get lost" in the syntax of their prayers can take comfort from his example!

The line of thought is roughly this:

Thanks be to God
> because he has brought us by new birth
>> to a confident hope of salvation
>>> which is for you who believe
>>> and are kept safely by God until it comes.

You rejoice in it,
> despite your present suffering
>> (which tests the reality of your faith
>> and will redound to the glory of Jesus Christ).

And you love him,
> despite not seeing him,

because even now you are receiving salvation—
> a salvation that was proclaimed by the prophets
>> (who did not themselves see it)
> but is now experienced by you.

Praise to God for the Hope of Salvation (1:3-5) Peter starts with an expression of praise that is exactly the same as the wording used in

Notes: **1:3** The Gk word translated "mercy" has a possible ambiguity about it. On the one hand, there is the normal understanding of the word to mean showing compassion to people who do not deserve it (for example, "although the man was guilty and the usual penalty was imprisonment, the judge had mercy and gave him a lighter sentence because of extenuating circumstances"). On the other hand, the word as used here reflects the Hebrew term *ḥesed,* which generally refers to the gracious conduct expected within a particular relationship (having made his covenant with the people of Israel, God can be relied on to show them his favor and to be faithful to them). Here, then, the thought is more of God's acting in accordance with his character and his promises. Since in 2:10 his thought refers to Gentiles being admitted to the covenant made centuries earlier with Israel and now renewed in Jesus, Peter's thinking here is probably the same. Nevertheless, within this context, God's action comes spontaneously out of his compassionate love rather than on the basis of his justice. (See Andersen 1986:41-88 for an important reassessment of the prevailing interpretation of *ḥesed.*)

2 Corinthians 1:3 and Ephesians 1:3. This shows that this form of words had become traditional in the church, probably widely used in prayer and praise in church meetings.

Two kinds of attitudes to this form of prayer coexist in the church today. Some people like to use existing, set forms of words. That they have been recited for centuries or authorized in a prayer book for use in worship has deep significance for them: their praise to God is a real part of that offered in the communion of saints in every age. At the same time, there is the danger that such praise can lack both spontaneity and living relevance to the concrete situation.

Other people eschew any kind of formal prayers because either they find the repetition of familiar forms of words makes them boring and meaningless or they feel that the Spirit should inspire more spontaneous expressions of praise. At the same time, there is the danger that they might fall unconsciously into weak patterns of prayer, characterized by such nonsense as "Lord, we just want to praise you, Lord, for this, and, Lord, we just want to ask you for that, and, Lord, we ask you to bless so-and-so."

Peter's expression of praise here shows that he uses familiar church language to provide the framework for his prayer and that he relates what he says to the specific situation at the moment.

Peter proclaims that God is worthy of praise, and already in the way in which he names God we can see one of the reasons for praising him: He is *the God and Father of our Lord Jesus Christ*. In a similar prayer in Luke 1:68, Zechariah describes him as the Lord God of Israel, and his

---

Hope is one of the most characteristic terms in 1 Pet (1:3, 13, 21; 3:5, 15). Peter seems to use it as a synonym for *faith* (3:5, 15). It expresses the strong element of looking forward to what God will do in the future that is present in this letter. Yet this does not mean that Peter lacks the strong emphasis on present faith and experience of God's grace that is typical of the New Testament generally. Rather, in a situation of hostility and consequent uncertainty the hope of future deliverance becomes especially significant.

It is not surprising that Peter here sees the resurrection of Jesus rather than the cross as the saving event that guarantees our future. It is theologically incorrect to lay all the stress on the cross and to ignore the resurrection (and of course vice versa).

Peter's use of *inheritance* further exemplifies the typology that occurs so often in this letter, which draws a parallel between the experiences of the people of God in the Old Testament and the new people of God. This implies that the church replaces Israel as the recipient of God's promises—that the promises of a "spiritual land" are the real promises.

praise includes what God has done and will do for the nation whom he specially chose to be his people. But here the praise is for the God who sent Jesus and who has revealed himself as the Father of Jesus. Although the Jews already knew of God as Father, the full revelation of the intimacy of this relationship came to those who saw how it was realized in Jesus and came to understand that they were admitted to the same relationship. Jesus himself is described as *Lord*. This Old Testament name and description of God the Father is here transferred to Jesus.

Now we come to the "reasoned statement" that expresses why God is worthy of praise. Three ideas are packed together in the first part of the statement:

1. God acts in mercy (see 2:10). Having made promises to his people in Old Testament times, God now acts in accordance with them to show his love and compassion. Peter refers to God's mercy as great, reflecting Old Testament language (Ex 34:6; Num 14:18; Ps 86:5, 15).

2. God brings believers to a new birth. The beginning of the Christian life is expressed in various ways in the New Testament, and one of them is the thought of new life. Jesus spoke to Nicodemus of the need for a new birth or a birth from above. This same concept is present here. Becoming a Christian is like being born into the world, only this time a new spiritual life commences in the person who has already experienced physical birth. The concept emphasizes that the source of life is outside ourselves and lies wholly with God whose Word engenders life (1:23). The metaphor is not pushed beyond the thought of the engendering of life, the action of the Father alone being envisaged with no thought being given to any metaphorical equivalent of a mother.

3. Believers have a living hope. To be born is to enter into existence in a new world. Physical birth brings us into a world that will eventually perish. Spiritual birth is into a world where there is hope for the future. *Hope* is a key word in the letter and sets the tone for Peter's intense concern with the future of Christians living in a hostile world (see 1:13, 21; 3:5, 15). When Peter calls it a *living* hope, it is not clear whether he means "a hope of life" or "a genuine (as opposed to an empty) hope." Either interpretation makes good sense, for clearly he has the real hope of a new life in mind.

But what is hope? It is the conviction that something will happen in the future. But for that conviction to exist there has to be some kind of basis. If I hope—in the sense of having the conviction—that the sun will rise tomorrow morning, that conviction does not come from knowledge of the future but rather from the fact that every morning the sun has risen and from the reasonable inference that it will continue to do so. (Yet there is the element of uncertainty: the end of the world *might* happen tomorrow.)

So too the hope of future life rests on the fact that God raised Jesus from the dead and on the reasonable inference that, if God raised Jesus, he will also raise those who trust in Jesus. "Inference" is, however, the wrong word, because Peter would call it the "promise" made by God. The strength of the hope rests on the reliability of the fact *and* the promise. The fact is certainly one that is accepted by faith. I believe that Jesus rose from the dead, although I may not be able to prove it in a universally acceptable manner. The promise is also accepted by faith. The New Testament writers express its centrality by speaking of God on occasion as *the God who raised Jesus from the dead.* Thus hope is a part of faith and a consequence of it.

But there is more to be said. The New Testament clearly teaches that eternal life is a present experience of Christians. Already in this life the new birth leads to a new life. The element of hope concerns whether this new experience will continue beyond physical death, beyond, that is to say, the limits of human experience and observation. There is thus somewhat of a tension in the New Testament between the future experience of salvation in all its fullness—free from the limitations imposed by the mortal body—and the genuine experience of salvation here and now. Part of our certainty regarding the future, therefore, arises not only from our trust in God's promises for the future but from our present experience of God fulfilling his promises to us. Out of the reality of our present Christian experience arises our conviction that our hope in God is not empty and delusory.

In the rest of the sentence Peter expands in two ways what he has said about the hope of the Christian:

1. He defines it as an *inheritance.* This word has a different emphasis in the New Testament from what it has in ordinary usage. Now we tend to use the word for the property that a son or other legal heir receives

on the death of his father. This legal right may well have been expressed in a will. But the New Testament uses the word to express more the legal claim which the heir already has on the property even while the father is still alive. The younger son in the parable of Jesus asked his father, who was very much alive, to give him the part of the estate that already "belonged" to him. To have something as an inheritance, then, indicates that we are already named in the will as those who are appointed to inherit it and that, in a sense, our name is already on it. Peter is underlining the fact that the content of the living hope is already destined for us.

A second nuance in the word *inheritance* is important. When the people of Israel were marching through the desert from Egypt to the land of Canaan, Moses spoke to them about *the land the LORD your God is giving you to possess as your inheritance* (Deut 15:4). They were not yet in the land, but God had promised it to them. They could think of it as being already theirs. When the same term is used in the New Testament, it conveys the idea of a promised land which is prepared for God's people: the heavenly territory that God has destined for them. Three adjectives are used to describe the promised inheritance: imperishable (see 1:23; 3:4), pure and unfading (see 5:4). These words all express its eternal character in contrast to earthly possessions and thus indicate its infinite worth. Finally, Peter says that this inheritance is kept safely by God in heaven for his people. It is like a treasure laid up in heaven, a thought that possibly echoes the teaching of Jesus in Luke 12:22-40.

2. It is not much use, however, to carefully preserve an inheritance if the heir is not going to live to receive it. So, in view of the tribulations that they are facing, Peter reassures his readers that they are being kept safely by God. They are like a fort which is garrisoned to keep it safe from enemy attacks (compare 2 Thess 3:3; Jude 24); God will protect them by his power from the hostile attacks of evil. At the same time their faith is shielding them. This comment shows that God's power does not work automatically, regardless of the attitude of the Christian. It is as Christians trust in God that they experience his power to protect them.

Here, then, is a paradox that we cannot resolve. It would go beyond biblical teaching to say that our faith is wholly due to the power of God, and it would be equally mistaken to say that God's power comes into action in our lives only as a result of our faith. It might be more true to say that God's power and our faith are two sides of the same coin, but to say this is not to explain how they are related. We can make a rough analogy with the way that children depend on their father to protect them. The good father's care goes beyond what his children expect and is shown even when they are not showing an attitude of trust but one of folly. Equally, the children draw courage from knowing that their father is always there in order to venture on their own even when their dad is not active. In the same way we see a certain lack of precision about the relationship between divine power and human faith, but the fact that we cannot define the relationship more closely is no argument for denying the existence of the two factors.

Peter then expresses the time frame of God's protection of believers: They are being kept until the revelation of salvation at the End. There are three points to note here:

1. The content of Christian hope is *salvation.* Like *peace* (1:2), the word *salvation* encompasses all that God gives to his people (see 1:9, 10; 2:2; 3:21; 4:18). It contains the ideas of rescue from danger, healing from illness, deliverance from the threat of death and entering into a state of well-being.

2. Peter refers to the future condition of Christians when they enter into the life of the world to come. Although the New Testament writers also speak of Christians as being already saved, the emphasis lies on the future state; present salvation is an anticipation of what we shall enjoy fully in the future. It is as if Peter were describing salvation as being like a new model of a car, sitting under wraps in a showroom and waiting for display on the day when it comes on sale. Christians, if the metaphor may be pressed, are people who are already enjoying test drives in advance of its official release.

3. This revelation of salvation will be made *in the last time.* This means the end of the world, when Christ himself will appear (1:7; 5:4). Peter speaks about it as something that could happen within the lifetime of his readers; otherwise there would be little point in referring to it at all.

The Testing of Faith (1:6-7) In the second part of this thanksgiving Peter brings out a further aspect of tension in Christian living. He has already drawn a contrast between the fulfillment of Christian hope and the present situation of living by faith. Now he shows how this situation is one of rejoicing despite suffering and of testing in hope of future approval. He begins by noting how Christians can and do rejoice in their present situation because of the hope that lies ahead of them.

Before he explains its basis, Peter comments that joy is possible despite present suffering. First, he makes it clear (1) that such suffering is a possibility from time to time rather than a permanent experience (he is not suggesting that the Christian life is a continuous succession of painful experiences), (2) that suffering takes place only if it is necessary because God allows it to happen, and (3) that suffering is only *for a little while*. This last point is one of the hardest things to believe when a person is in pain; every moment seems an eternity. Peter means, no doubt, that the period of suffering is short compared with the eternal duration of future salvation (see 5:10), but he may also be saying that suffering will not last long in absolute terms.

Second, Peter says that the suffering comes in the form of *trials*. This is an ambiguous word that can mean "trial" or "temptation." A trial is a test to see if something can stand up to strain. A temptation is an attempt to destroy something. In the Bible it includes the idea of an appeal to yield to a sinful desire. God does not tempt us, encouraging us to yield to sin, but he can use the devil's temptations as means of testing the strength of our will. Temptation can take the form of pleasure in doing something that is forbidden (Adam and Eve yielded to the desire to enjoy forbidden fruit), but it can also entice us to do something

---

1:6 *In this* is ambiguous. It could signify: (1) "In whom [namely, God]." The relative pronoun would then point back to God (or possibly Jesus) in 1:3, which is a rather distant point of reference; (2) "In which [time]." The thought is then that Christians will rejoice (translating the verb as a present with a future reference) at the end of time. This view is supported by Goppelt (1978:98-99; compare Michaels 1988:25), who points out that the verb used here (Gk *agalliaomai*) is used of "rejoicing greatly"; that there is a contrast between present rejoicing (Gk *chairō*) and future *great joy* in 4:13; and that 1:8 can and should also be interpreted of future joy. However, the tense of the verb is present, and elsewhere in the New Testament it is used for present joy (Acts 2:46; 16:34). I prefer the view (3) "In which [circumstance]" (see 3:18; 4:4; Grudem 1988:60). The point is then not a contrast between present suffering and future fullness of joy but rather the paradox of greatly rejoicing now despite suffering.

The important qualifying phrase "if necessary" (Gk *ei deon*) is hidden in the *may have had to* of NIV, obscuring the implication that suffering happens only if God allows it to be used by him to forward his purposes.

When *gold* is said to be perishable, the thought is not that the fire can destroy it (fire

to avoid painful consequences. In persecution the devil entices us to give up our faith for fear of suffering ridicule or physical harm of some kind. Peter has this attack in mind, and later he refers to it as a *fiery trial.*

Third, Peter indicates the purpose that God has in allowing his people to suffer: Trials test the faith of God's people. Peter draws an analogy with the purifying of metals. Gold is a precious metal, but it can be mixed with impurities, which lower its value and spoil its beauty. Even though it is a precious metal, it needs to be refined. And so it is subjected to the intense heat of fire in a crucible, where impurities rise to the surface of the melted gold and are skimmed off by the goldsmith. God values Christian faith much more than gold, which, although precious, belongs to this world and will ultimately be destroyed. Faith, too, must be refined so that it will be genuine and thus redound to the glory of Christ.

A Christian's faith contains human, sinful elements. In the crucible of testing these other elements are purged away, leaving the purified faith which survives the test. Then, at his coming, Christ's glory will be increased by the presence of believers whose faith has stood up to every trial and test. A Christian's faith, then, is literally *found* at the coming of Christ and leads to *praise, glory and honor.* This could mean either praise for the person who displays the faith or that the faithful person brings praise and honor to Christ. Both thoughts are possible. Peter teaches clearly that the faithfulness of Christians leads to rejoicing when the glory of Christ is revealed (4:13) and that faithful Christians are called to eternal glory in Christ (5:10). It is probably the latter thought which is

---

can only melt it) but rather simply to draw a contrast between faith and gold as respectively lasting and not lasting into the next world.

1:7 *Your faith may be proved genuine and may result* is literally "the genuineness of your faith may be found." The word translated "genuine" is an adjective and means "the [successfully] tested part" of your faith. The thought may be that faith is tested, as by fire, and what survives the destruction of impurities is the successfully tested part. This implies that fire tries to destroy the faith, just as it destroys the impurities, but the faith successfully resists, just as gold withstands fire while its impurities do not.

The verb "find" (Gk *heuriskō*) is used of the way in which people and their qualities are laid bare before God at the judgment and publicly shown to be of a certain kind (see 2 Cor 5:3; Phil 3:9; 2 Pet 3:14; for Old Testament usage see Ps 17:3; Dan 6:22).

The Second Coming of Christ is here spoken of as *when Jesus Christ is revealed* (1 Cor 1:7; 2 Thess 1:7), emphasizing that the One who is presently hidden from the world and who was seen by only a few people during his first coming will be revealed openly so that all will see him in his glory as the Son of God. The implied contrast between hiddenness and revelation is developed in 1:8-9.

present here (compare Dan 12:3; Rom 2:7, 10, 29). Christians will receive recognition from God; their faith in him will be vindicated. And this will happen when Jesus Christ is revealed—at his Second Coming (compare 4:13). Because this is the purpose of testing, Christians can rejoice despite their trials.

The Hidden Presence of Christ (1:8-9) Peter has proclaimed that the Christian life is one of hope despite the fact that our future salvation is not yet revealed and that it is also a life of rejoicing despite present testing of faith. He says, finally, that it is a life of believing despite not yet seeing the Savior.

This last comment brings out the intensely personal character of Christian faith. What matters in the end is not so much the fact of future salvation or of future praise but rather the hope of seeing Christ. Unlike the original eyewitnesses (including Peter himself) the readers have never seen Christ in the flesh. Despite this they love him. Here is the deepest expression of the Christian's relationship to Christ. It goes beyond feeling personal emotional ties and expresses a commitment similar to that expressed by the word *believe,* but it brings out, as *believe* does not, the warmth of the personal emotion that the believer has for Christ in response to the love which Christ first showed to the believer.

The point is then partially repeated to bring out a fresh lesson. The readers do not now see Jesus. Here they are like Peter, who could no longer see the Christ whom he once saw. But both Peter and the readers could nevertheless be filled with unutterable joy through their relationship to Jesus. The language is piled up, intensifying the feeling of joy beyond expression in words and infused with heavenly glory. This joy already shares in the quality of heavenly joy.

1:8 The grammatical form of the phrase *though you have not seen him* suggested to Windisch (1951:53) and Selwyn (1947:131) that Peter was contrasting the experience of his readers with his own past experience of actually seeing Jesus. This is dubious, and in any case the main contrast is between the present experience of the readers and their future hope.

Peter may simply mean *glorious joy* as when we talk of a "glorious victory," using the adjective simply as a superlative. The language is so strong that Goppelt (1978:103-4) argues that what Peter is describing is not a present experience but a future one at the appearance of Christ (see 1:6 note). But it is difficult to justify translating the present tense "you rejoice" as a future when it stands parallel to the unequivocal present tense "you love." Furthermore, the time reference of a present participle is normally the same as that of the main verb to

Finally, Peter adds somewhat loosely that Christians are already receiving the goal of their faith, their salvation. If salvation is future in 1:5, here Peter speaks of it as something that believers receive here and now.

The picture of the Christian life presented by Peter in these opening verses is characterized by hope in what God will do in the future. Christians, he says, look forward to salvation in the world to come. Their lives ought to have a forward-looking and other-worldly dimension that is often lacking among contemporary Christians. As we go through 1 Peter, we will, of course, need to keep in mind Peter's attitude toward the existing world. But we already note that Peter's strong stress on the future does address questions to us. Have we lost the future dimension from the life of the individual Christian and of the church? Have we grown used to a situation in which the coming of Christ and the revelation of salvation do not fall within our expectations? True, we believe in the future hope in principle, but has it lost its importance as a factor in our daily living? And, as a result, do we lay too much stress on salvation now, both in our own lives and in the life of the world, and too little on what Christ has yet to bring?

The Prophecies of Salvation (1:10-12) The use of prayers to exhort the congregation, and even to educate the Lord himself, is not exactly unknown in the church today, and those who adopt such practices can claim excellent precedents. This section, 1:3-12, started off as an expression of thanks to God for the living hope that Christians enjoy, but by the time Peter reaches this paragraph he no longer is giving the reasons for praising God. He is teaching. In fact, from verse 6 onward, he has been giving a theological explanation of his readers' situation in relation to their future salvation. In Peter's defense, it may be argued that

---

which it is subordinated. So it is difficult syntactically to take the meaning to be "you do not see him now but believe in him and you will rejoice." The alternative rendering "you will not see him but believe in him and you will rejoice" produces theological nonsense.

1:9 The same problem of tense arises here as in verse 8. Since salvation is a future entity in verse 5, the temptation to take this verse in a future sense is strong. Salvation is then the ultimate goal of our present faith. Nevertheless, salvation is by no means purely future; the readers have already begun to enjoy its blessings.

Goal (Gk *telos*) has been well defined as "the outcome or destiny which awaits people in accordance with their nature." Salvation is the appropriate outcome of faith.

Souls is probably a Hebraism and is equivalent to a personal pronoun. It refers to the personal or spiritual center of our existence.

he is not saying a prayer but writing a letter; with the slowness of dictation it would not be too difficult to lose the original thread and digress.

We now have a theological discussion of an important part of biblical interpretation. One of our modern temptations as Christians is to read the Scriptures of the Old Testament as if they had originally been written as a Christian book. We take the prophecies as referring primarily to the coming of Jesus and the establishment of the church. No doubt we are aware that the main theme of the Old Testament is the story of the people of Israel and their relationship with God through many centuries. Nevertheless, essentially we see the Old Testament story as preparation for what has happened since Jesus came. Old Testament scholars insist that we must read the Old Testament in its own right, as the history of the people of Israel, and understand first of all what the prophets were saying to their contemporaries.

This approach has the merits of taking the Old Testament seriously as history and of understanding the prophets as people with messages for their own people in their own time. But even many Jews themselves, by the time of Christ, were trying to bring the Old Testament up to date. They reapplied its laws to their own situation and worked out in greater detail how they were to be kept. They were also reading the prophecies and asking: Can these writings be interpreted in such a way that we can see that they apply to us? At least one Jewish group, the Essenes at Qumran, found the details of its own history foretold in various prophetic writings.

Over and against this kind of activity Christians made a bid to take over the Old Testament as a Christian book, and this passage is of crucial importance in explaining how they did so. One interesting question,

---

1:11 *The time and circumstances* is one interpretation of a Greek phrase (literally, "what [thing or person] or what [kind of] time") which could also be translated "the person and the circumstances." On this alternative translation the prophets were enquiring about the identity of the person whose coming had been revealed to them as well as about the time or circumstances of his coming (for a convincing argument in favor of this translation see Grudem 1988:74-75).

The foretelling of the future is ascribed to the activity of the Spirit, who is here called the *Spirit of Christ*. This description ties in with the fact that the Spirit is elsewhere called the Spirit of Christ because he is poured out by Christ on the church and because his activity is concerned with the work of Christ in the church and with bringing glory to Christ. Although the Spirit is regarded as not being given to Christ to bestow on his people until

which commentators on the whole tend to leave unanswered, is why Peter felt it necessary to discuss this point at all. Was he attempting to deal with people, like the Qumran sect, who disputed the Christian "takeover bid" for the Old Testament as Christian Scripture? Or is he simply attempting to convince his readers that salvation really is for them?

When Peter speaks of *the grace that was to come to you,* he is describing what the prophets said from a Christian point of view. Their messages, or at least some of them, had a future orientation. It is not necessary to assume that Peter meant that all prophecy was specifically concerned with the future grace of God, but he recognizes (what is incontestable) that some prophecies were about what God would do in the future for those who would then be alive. Peter assumes that this theme was what God had done in the coming of Christ (and what he would continue to do) for those who believed.

He then states that the prophets asked God about the significance of the message which they had received from him. The prophets are envisaged as engaging in dialog with God. We know that some of them did talk to God about the message that they were given to deliver. (Jeremiah is the prime example of a person who expostulated with God about his painful message to the people.) But again he puts it from a Christian angle by saying that they asked God concerning *this salvation;* his choice of this phrase is dictated by the fact that he himself had used the word *salvation* in the previous verses to describe God's gift to Christians.

Peter explains more closely what the prophets did by saying that they enquired in what time and circumstances the prophecies would be fulfilled, which they had been given by the Spirit concerning the sufferings

his exaltation (Acts 2:33), it is legitimate to regard the Spirit, who already bears witness to Christ in the Old Testament Scriptures, as the Spirit of Christ. Although the Old Testament prophets themselves make little reference to the source of their inspiration, that their prophecy was due to the Spirit coming upon them is frequently mentioned both in Jewish writings and in the New Testament itself (for example, Mk 12:36; Acts 1:16; Heb 3:7; 9:8; 10:15; 2 Pet 1:21).

For prophets who discussed their message with God, see Jer 12:1-6; 14:11-16; 15:15-21; for the problem of when fulfillment would happen, see Hab 2:1-3; Dan 9:24-25; 12:6-7; 4 Ezra 4:33, 45, 51; and, in the New Testament, Acts 1:6-8. Note that the point here is not explicitly that the prophets themselves were longing to see the period of fulfillment (as in Lk 10:23-24).

destined for Christ and the glories to follow. Later Peter will cite phrases from Isaiah 53 as prophecies of the suffering of Jesus, and obviously this passage is typical of what he has in mind at this point. The prophets wanted to know in what way this kind of prophecy would be fulfilled.

Interestingly, Peter speaks of prophetic activity as a *service,* a means of helping God's people. Peter's answer to the prophets' enquiry is that the prophets were told by God that their message was not to do with themselves but with a later generation. This future generation is described, again from Peter's own perspective, as *you,* the readers. We do not need to envisage God as actually describing the Christian church to the prophets; it is sufficient that they were told that their prophecies would be fulfilled in the future "in those days and at that time" (Joel 3:1).

What the prophets foretold is then identified as the message proclaimed to the readers by those who evangelized them in the power of the Holy Spirit. This tightly packed sentence contains a number of thoughts:

1. What the prophets foretold is now the content of the evangelistic message of the church. From Paul's summary of the gospel in 1 Corinthians 15:3-5 we gain full confirmation of this point. The gospel, as proclaimed by him and by the other apostles, was: "Christ died for our sins *according to the Scriptures,* he was buried, he was raised on the third day *according to the Scriptures,* and he appeared to Peter and then to the Twelve." This message, although couched in the form of a historical report, is backed up from the Scriptures: his death for our sins and his resurrection on the third day were prophesied in the Scriptures and thus are the fulfillment of these prophecies.

2. The Holy Spirit sent from heaven enabled the evangelists to preach

---

The object of prediction is literally "the sufferings to/for Christ and the glories after these things." On the traditional view the phrase refers to the sufferings destined for the Messiah and the glorious events (the resurrection and exaltation, the Second Coming and so on) to follow. But the phrase is cumbersome, and Selwyn (1947:136-37) argues that it means "the sufferings of the Christward way and the glorious experiences to follow"—that is, the sufferings undergone by those who follow Christ and their experiences of glory thereafter. This gives an appropriate interpretation of the phrase in the context of a letter that is very much concerned with the sufferings of Christians; yet, where are the sufferings of Christians prophesied in the Old Testament?

1:12 *Themselves* probably means the prophets and their own generation. Peter corrects this message. This is a reference to the coming of the Spirit at Pentecost. The Holy Spirit is of course the šame as the Spirit of Christ, so that Peter says, in effect, that the Spirit who inspired the prophets also inspired the evangelists and gave them insight into the true meaning of the prophets. The activity of the Spirit thus creates the connection between the giving of prophecy in the past and the interpretation of prophecy now. Through their understanding of the prophetic Scriptures the early Christians came to understand more fully the significance of the coming of Jesus and had the categories to explain his person and his work. For example, they recognized that he was the Suffering Servant of Yahweh and that his death was like that of a Passover lamb.

3. It is probable, though less obvious, that Peter recognizes the prophecies about the coming of Jesus as being fulfilled, not just for the Jews but also for the Gentiles, because the *you* whom he addresses were, at least in part, a Gentile Christian audience.

4. He adds the interesting statement that *the angels long to look into these things.* We should presume that angels are ignorant of certain things (Mk 13:32; Rom 16:25; 1 Cor 2:6-9), and that they long to know more as they see the fulfillment of God's purposes (Lk 15:10; Rom 8:19). The remark underlines how fortunate are those living to see and experience personally the fulfillment of the prophecies (compare Mt 13:16-17; Lk 10:23-24).

In summary, then, Peter points out that the Holy Spirit has revealed that the readers are living in the time when the prophecies of salvation have been fulfilled. This confirms their Christian experience and gives a firm foundation for their future hope. He provides a rationale for the relevance of the prophetic writings to these Christians' situation, and thus emphasizes their privileged position.

---

the assumption that the prophets were concerned only with their own generation, as if God could not give them messages intended for later generations. An alternative interpretation of this passage was put forward by Selwyn (1947:259-68). He argued that the prophets in question were not the Old Testament prophets but Christian prophets in the early church and that their prophecies were not about the suffering and glory of Christ himself but about the sufferings and subsequent glorious experiences of the Christians in Asia Minor. This is an attractive explanation of the passage, but it has been subjected to strong criticism by other scholars. Selwyn's idea refers to an activity by Christian prophets for which there is little other evidence and draws rather a strong temporal contrast between the time of the prophets and the time of the evangelists.

What, then, has this passage to say to modern readers?

1. It reminds us that from a Christian point of view the Old Testament is not just a time-bound book, with prophetic messages meant purely for the original readers. Important though this aspect is, the Old Testament is rightly recognized to have a future orientation. Specific passages look ahead to the coming of the Messiah and the establishment of the church, and we will interpret some passages wrongly if we insist on finding in them a message purely for the prophets' own times.

2. There is a continuity in revelation. The church can take over the Old Testament as part of its Scriptures; indeed, it must do so. The same Holy Spirit was active in both Old Testament and New Testament times, bearing witness to Christ. The Old Testament contains expressions of the will and purpose of God which are valid at all times.

3. If the prophets had to learn that some of God's messages were meant for others and not for themselves, perhaps we need to learn that not all of Scripture is meant to speak directly to us nor written with us in mind. It is true that "all Scripture is God-breathed and is useful in teaching" (2 Tim 3:16), but we should differentiate between passages written for God's people in general and passages written for specific people with a primary application to them and only a secondary application to us. For example, the prophecy of Obadiah is concerned with a very specific situation in the history of the Israelites and their neighbors in Edom. The details of the message have a strictly local application. If we are to hear in it a word from God for us, we will only perceive it properly when we observe what general principles of divine teaching come to particular expression in it and reapply the message to ourselves. To take a trivial example in this letter, *she who is in Babylon, chosen together with you, sends you her greetings, and so does my son Mark* (5:13) conveys a message to Peter's original readers and not to us. The message of the verse to us is an indirect one, an example of the way in which we should express our sympathy and love for Christians sharing in the same difficulties and trials as ourselves.

☐ The Basic Characteristics of Christian Living (1:13—2:10)

Snowstorms and violent weather mark the winters of the Cairngorm Mountains near my home in Scotland. Almost every year some unfortunate climbers who venture out on them at that season come to grief, not because they are inexperienced climbers, but because they set out ill-prepared for the weather. Every year warnings are given that the mountains are treacherous in the winter. While they are safe for fully equipped and experienced climbers, they can be fatal for the ill-equipped.

Peter's readers were likely to face opposition from a hostile society round about them. In the second part of the letter Peter will tell them what they are to do when they are actually in the world and facing hostility, but in this first part he instructs them on how to be prepared and equipped spiritually for what lies ahead of them. The Scottish preacher Murdo Ewan Macdonald used to speak of the necessity of having "adequate internal resources." This is the heart of Peter's message in this section of his letter, which is concerned with the personal lives of Christians and how they are to behave individually in relation to God (1:13-21) and to other Christians (1:22—2:3) and collectively in the church (2:4-10).

The mood of the letter changes at this point. Throughout the preceding section the indicative mood has been used almost exclusively to offer a factual statement of the situation of Christians as they experience the grace of God that leads to salvation. From this point onward imperatives become dominant, and the tone is one of command. This order of indicative followed by imperative is not a chance one. First must come the gospel and only then the response to it. First we hear of what God has graciously done for us, and then of what we are to do in obedience to him. The latter is not possible except when it is made so by the former.

The teaching given here is not directly related to the theme of hostility, and my assessment of it in terms of being ready to face opposition is based on its context in this letter. It is in fact general teaching that would be appropriate to Christians in any situation, and particularly appropriate to new Christians. Not surprisingly, some scholars have detected here the kind of teaching that might be given on the occasion of baptism, the occasion of the entry of new converts into the membership of the church.

Hope and Obedience (1:13-21) The instruction falls into three sections. The first section focuses on the character of Christian living as it is derived from the Christian's attitude to God. It is a call to a life of hope and obedience to God. This involves turning aside from the former way of life to a new life of holiness based on God's character. Christians must remember that God their Father is still their judge and that the cost of their redemption was the blood of Christ.

The thoughts developed here have their origins in the story of the people of Israel, redeemed from Egypt and called to a life of holiness. Here the church is said to be like Israel. Later on the church will be virtually identified as the new Israel of God.

The Vigor of Hope (1:13) Just as Paul not infrequently gives doctrinal teaching about the nature of Christian salvation and then goes on to say "Therefore, you must live in such and such a way" (Rom 12:1; Col 3:1), so too Peter bases his practical teaching for Christian living on the doctrine contained in his initial thanksgiving section with his *therefore* in verse 13. The connection is quite direct. The initial theme in 1:3 was the living hope that has been given to the readers. If this is God's promise to them, then they must actually live in hope. To live by hope is to derive a sense of purpose out of the goal set before us.

The object of our hope is an inviting one: the grace of God (compare 1:10), which will be bestowed when Jesus Christ is revealed. It is worth noting again that Peter constantly thinks of what will be bestowed by God in the future at the Second Coming of Jesus. More and greater blessings are in store for Christians than we at present enjoy, and one of the incentives for Christian living should be our sense of anticipation of what God will give to us at the End.

Although God gives his grace to Christians here and now, the particular experience of grace that Peter has in mind here will be known only at the end of the journey. Christians will not reach the goal without living appropriately. They are summoned to vigorous activity. They are to have minds that are prepared for action. The Greek idiom used here (and lost in the rather bland NIV translation) is the ancient equivalent of "Roll up

Notes: 1:13 *Prepare for action* is literally "gird up your loins" and refers to the practice of tucking up flowing garments around the waist in order to be free for action (Lk 17:8; Acts 12:8). The phrase is used metaphorically in Luke 12:35 and Ephesians 6:14.

Mind is the center of understanding that produces thoughts and resolves, the power of

your sleeves and get down to hard work!" The language can in fact be traced back to Exodus 12:11 where the Israelites, about to leave Egypt, are told to eat the Passover, dressed and equipped to start out on the long and tough journey without delay. So too Peter's readers are to set out on their journey to the "Promised Land" and must be ready for action. To go out as Christians on pilgrimage through the world demands vigor.

The readers also need to be self-controlled. This command is repeated throughout the letter (4:7; 5:8). Literally it means "be sober." Intoxication befuddles the mind, taking away the ability to make sharp, prompt and rational decisions and inducing a sense of spurious well-being that can be totally out of touch with reality. This is true of a variety of drugs and alcohol. Peter's command here is without question to be taken on the literal level, as 4:3-4 makes clear.

A powerful tradition of biblical interpretation in evangelical Christianity has insisted that the New Testament teaching strongly implies abstinence from alcohol as the appropriate way to fulfil this command in the circumstances of the modern world. Recognition of the way in which even limited indulgence in alcohol impairs motor skills and the ability to make rational decisions, as well as its detrimental effects on health simply reinforces it. Nevertheless, today many more Christians, in conformity to the ways of the world around them, tolerate the moderate consumption of alcohol than used to be the case. Let them consider more seriously the teaching of this letter and ask themselves whether the Christian ideals of holiness, of preparedness for vigorous living and of witness against the evils of society do not suggest that abstinence is the better way.

But Peter of course is not commenting purely on the literal level. He is concerned with the broad danger of not being alert to spiritual realities, the failure to recognize temptation as temptation, the failure to assess situations from the Christian point of view and so on. Some observe that when Paul visited Athens he saw not a collection of beautiful

---

rational judgment which can be swayed by outside factors such as the appeal of *evil desires* (1:14).

Fully is linked to *set your hope* in NIV, but it should possibly be linked rather with *be self-controlled* (compare 2 Tim 4:5 for the thought).

pieces of architecture and sculpture but the temples and images of the pagan gods who were worshiped there. His reaction was not to admire the beauty but to preach the gospel. We similarly need to see the world and our own duty in it realistically.

Obedience and Holiness (1:14-16) The practical expression of the new way of life centered on hope, or rather on the God in whom we hope, is developed in this section both negatively and positively. As a kind of heading we have the phrase *as obedient children.* Christians are God's children, who know him as their Father (1:17). In the biblical world the characteristic quality associated with a father was care for his children (Ps 103:13; Mt 7:9-11), and the corresponding characteristic of children was obedience to their father. Obedience to God signifies negatively that his children will not go on living as they used to do, molded by whatever their sinful desires suggest. The readers used to be characterized by a pagan ignorance of God (compare Acts 17:30; Eph 4:18; 1 Thess 4:5). Consequently, they did not realize that their desires were evil. But now as God's children they have no excuse for ignorance or for conforming their lives to the pattern of the sinful world.

Positively, obedience to God necessitates becoming holy like him. Whatever the original history of this word, it came to express the essential character of God himself, summed up in such terms as purity, truth, sincerity, righteousness and opposition to evil. The holiness of God himself is both the pattern for holiness and the reason for holiness. Peter quotes from Leviticus 11:44 (= 19:2), a command that God directed to the people of Israel as they journeyed to the Promised Land. It referred

---

1:14 *As* has the force "since you ought to be." *Obedient* children is literally "children of obedience," a Hebrew form of expression (see Eph 2:2). Obedience is one of the key thoughts of the letter (1:2, 22; 3:6; Frederick 1975).

The verb translated *do not conform* suggests the idea of being forced into a mold and adopting its shape. Significantly, the same word is used elsewhere in the New Testament only in Romans 12:2. J. B. Lightfoot argued that it meant "to follow the capricious guidance of" (Selwyn 1947:141). Greek students will note that the form of the verb is a participle used as an imperative. This usage, which is frequent in the letter, was identified by D. Daube as a Hebrew idiom (Selwyn 1947:466-78), but it may well be simply an example of Hellenistic Greek (Salom 1963).

NIV rightly interprets "desires" here as *evil desires.* The Greek word is ethically neutral and can refer to good desires (compare the use of the verb in 1:12), but is more frequently used of evil desires, especially in the areas of sex, greed and violence (2:11; 4:2-3).

1:15 For the thematic significance of holiness in 1 Peter see especially Elliott 1966.

to their character as God's people in keeping his commands. *Holy*, therefore, includes the sense of belonging to God, a people marked off and separate from the world by their way of life.

Peter does not feel compelled to justify applying this command to the members of the church. Although they are in large part Gentiles, they have come into the people of God. What was said to Israel in the Old Testament is now applicable to them. To be sure, the way in which the command is to be kept has altered. In Leviticus God was concerned with the ritual of the sacrificial system as well as with ethical requirements. But Peter freshly applies it in accordance with the basic principle of living in a way that is appropriate for God's people.

Let us remember that holiness affects not only our personal relationship to God but all of our relationships. It affects *all* you do (literally "your conduct"), and Peter is greatly interested in this theme (2:12; 3:1, 2, 16; compare with the corresponding verb in 1:17). Every other time Peter uses the noun, it is in the context of the public behavior of Christians. Peter is concerned that the way in which Christians live should testify to their faith in God, show the character of God and witness to the gospel; the behavior of Christians should be an incentive for other people to believe.

Fear and Faith (1:17-21) God is the One who judges everybody according to their works and who does so quite impartially, without favoring one or another. Christians are people who pray for help from this God as their Father (1:2). The prayer that Jesus taught his disciples and that was used in the early church addresses God by this name (Lk

---

1:17 The Greek is literally "if you call on the One who judges . . . as father, live in fear." At first sight this translation seems to place the emphasis on the wrong phrase, and we would expect rather "if the Father you call on is the One who judges . . . , live in fear." In other words, we would expect the motive for the fear to lie in the character of God as judge rather than as Father. The correct interpretation, however, is given by Selwyn (1947:142-43). The point is that our reverence for God should arise out of the fact that he is our Father, since reverence for fathers as such is a basic biblical idea. Hence the meaning is more like: "If you call upon the One who judges . . . as Father, do not think that this means that you can ignore his character as judge; on the contrary, precisely because he is your Father you must reverence him."

Peter develops the character of God as Father in verses 18-20, which show that in his love he gave his Son to redeem us. Reverence is the proper response to God's mercy and forgiveness. Peter later develops the fact that God the Father judges his people in 4:17-19; there it becomes clear that Peter sees no tension between the judgment by which God

11:2; compare Rom 8:15; Gal 4:6; Eph 3:14). But those who address God in this way must remember who he is. As Father he does not cease to be judge. Christians are not in a position where it doesn't matter how they live because they believe in Christ and all will be forgiven at the last judgment. On the contrary, they should live in this world, filled with its temptations, with reverence for God in the face of his judgment.

Peter fleshes out what this attitude involves. If he talked about God as the Father who should be reverenced because he judges his people, Peter now introduces a deeper motive for Christian conduct in the fact of redemption. The picture is of people who were in bondage but have now been set free. The concept of redemption in the ancient world applied to a variety of contexts, including the emancipation of slaves from their masters and the release of prisoners of war. In the Old Testament the picture was used to describe how God set his people free from bondage in Egypt and brought them out to live in freedom in the Promised Land. Later the return of the exiles from Babylon was depicted in similar terms (Is 52:3). Redemption generally takes place by the payment of a ransom.

Peter uses the picture here to make a number of points:

1. The former state of the readers was one of bondage—bondage to a particular way of life inherited from their ancestors. For the Romans, ancestral traditions were praiseworthy, but not so for Peter. The way of life described in 1:14 and 4:2 was dictated by evil desires and belonged to the time when the readers were ignorant of God and his will. It stands in contrast to the new, holy way of life that is now expected of them

---

purifies his church and God's character as the faithful Creator who cares for his people in the midst of the trials that he allows them to suffer. In ancient thought judicial authority was associated with fatherhood, so that it is not strange for Jesus to speak of the Father as king and judge (Mt 18:23-35; compare Schrenk 1967).

The concept of God as judge (2:23; 4:5-6) is taken over by the New Testament from Judaism. Sometimes Christ is regarded as acting as judge but only by the authority of the Father (for his impartiality, see Acts 10:34; Rom 2:11; Eph 6:9; Col 3:25; for judgment by works, see Rom 2:6-16; 2 Cor 5:10; Rev 20:12-15).

1:19 Although the comparison between Christ and the Passover lamb is primary, an allusion to Isaiah 53:7 (compare 1 Pet 2:23) is also quite probable. The topic of redemption is excellently discussed by W. Haubeck (1985).

1:20 Peter makes use here of a pattern of thought, found elsewhere in the New Testament, which draws a contrast between the formulation of God's secret saving plan before the creation of the world and its actual open revelation now in the endtime (Rom 16:25-

(1:15). The old way of life is characterized as *empty*, lacking in purpose and leading to no good results (compare Eph 4:17).

2. Redemption from bondage was possible only by the payment of a ransom price. Peter wants to emphasize the great cost involved, so he points out that the ransom was not paid with precious metals like silver and gold, which despite their durability are not of lasting worth, but rather with the blood of Christ, which is genuinely costly. He contrasts material wealth and a person's life, and the contrast is enhanced because it was the lifeblood of Christ that was spilled.

The way in which Peter frames the thought makes it clear that the reminder is not so much of the redemption itself but rather of the cost of the redemption. Christians can easily take their redemption for granted. The way to avoid this attitude is by remembering its infinite cost.

3. The reference to blood indicates that Christ's was not just an ordinary death but rather a sacrificial death. Peter develops this important idea by comparing Christ's blood to the blood of a sacrificial animal that was unblemished as the Law required. Only top-quality animals were acceptable to God. The language suggests that Peter has the the lamb sacrificed in the Passover ritual in mind. Whatever the original significance of the ritual, by New Testament times the Passover sacrifice had come to be regarded as a means of atonement for sin.

Peter is saying that the readers were caught, with no possibility of escape, in a futile way of life that would end in condemnation from the Judge who judges everybody according to their works. Christ's self-offering to God as a sacrifice, however, constituted the ransom price by which they were set

26; Eph 3:5-6, 9-10; Col 1:26; 2 Tim 1:9-10; Tit 1:2-3; compare Mt 25:34). In other passages where this scheme is used, it is the plan of God that was foreknown or formulated; here it is Christ himself who is said to have been foreordained to act as Redeemer. This raises the theological question as to whether Peter thought that Christ was pre-existent before creation or merely that God's plan antedated creation. Elsewhere (except possibly in the difficult passage 2 Tim 1:9-10) the concern is purely with the formulation of God's plan and not with the pre-existence of Christ. Nevertheless, the contrast here between "was foreordained" and "was manifested" strongly suggests the appearance in the world of a pre-existent being. Peter uses the language of incarnation, but because he is not primarily concerned to give teaching about the person of Christ, he employs it allusively and somewhat obliquely.

In these last times is a unique phrase, literally "at end of the times." Peter appears to envisage a series of periods of time stretching backward to creation (and beyond?). It is at the end of this series that Christ has appeared (compare 1:5). The phrase means much the same as "at the end of the days" (Heb 1:2) or "at the last time" (Jude 18).

free from the old way of life and brought into the new life of the children of God. Christ's death as a sacrifice for sin set them free from the prospect of condemnation and enabled them to escape from the downward path.

Although his point has been adequately made, Peter goes further. He links the sacrificial death of Jesus with the plan of God: The coming of Christ took place in accordance with a divine plan, which was made even before the creation of the world. Christ is said to have been "foreknown" by God. This means God foreordained him to carry out a particular task. But Christ's actual appearance in the world to do this did not take place until *in these last times*. By this phrase Peter indicates that he regards the present time as part of the End. The coming of Jesus marks the beginning of the end times. The emphasis lies on the last phrase *for your sake*, as if the whole purpose of God was formulated and carried out especially for the readers.

Peter develops this last point in verse 21. He describes the readers as those who through Christ believe in God. They are the people who put their trust in God as the God who raised Jesus from the dead (Rom 4:24) and gave him a share in his glory (3:21-22; Acts 3:13). In this way Peter emphasizes that God accepted the sacrifice made by Christ and showed his acceptance by raising him to the place of supreme honor. Because they know God as the One who raised Christ, Christians can confidently put their faith in him. Thus God achieves his purpose: that the readers should direct their faith and their hope toward God. They hope implicitly that the God who raised and glorified Jesus will also raise them to eternal life and grant them a share in the same glory (5:10). Thus *through him,* namely Christ, the readers come to have this faith in God.

Nothing in this section requires much reinterpretation for the modern reader. But some explanation of ideas and their associations in the ancient world is necessary, for instance the way in which the Father is automatically thought of as a person to be reverenced and the meaning of redemption.

Redemption has become an impersonal term, used of the exchange

---

1:21 This verse explains more precisely why Peter said in verse 20 that Christ was revealed *for your sakes:* so that they might trust in God when they realized that he accepted Christ's redemptive sacrifice and raised him from the dead. Peter's point is not to say that Christ was revealed *only* for the sake of believers, as if his coming was intended to save

of coupons for goods, the recovery of items from a pawnshop and the like. The concept of liberation may speak more powerfully to the present generation, but it should be noted that this term may overstress the idea of political deliverance, which was not necessarily in Peter's mind, and understress the thought of the sacrifice made by Christ to atone for sin. It is a different question whether we are right to extrapolate from what Peter says to the concept of political liberation as being part—but no more than a part—of what God offers to people in Christ.

The more immediate question is whether this section plays its part in preparing Christians for life in the world: Does it furnish them with adequate internal resources? These verses inculcate attitudes of continuing faith and hope in God himself, which are based on what is known of God's will: that his people should be holy; that he, as the Father, is to be revered; that he purposes to redeem his people, lovingly and powerfully, in the sacrifice and resurrection of Jesus. These attitudes are still the basis for Christian confidence, based not on our own abilities or even on our faith but on the God in whom we trust.

Love and Purity (1:22—2:3) Time and again the weakness of the church in facing the problems of the world lies in its own internal dissension. The ecumenical movement in our time has drawn attention to the serious divisions between different Christian groups and continues to look for ways to bring them together. It should be obvious to everyone that the failure of Christians to agree on central issues impairs their witness, a failure so great that often churches cannot work together in the proclamation of the gospel. What is more worrying is the way in which Christians tend to divide over issues of peripheral importance, taking rigid stances in matters on which Scripture has nothing to say or is ambiguous. And more worrying still is the failure of Christians to love one another and so to create the atmosphere in which some progress might be made toward the resolution of conflicts.

Now admittedly Peter is writing here about the situation within a local

a limited number of people; rather Christ came in order that all people—including his readers who have already done so—might believe. The point would be clearer if we translated the verse like this: "He . . . was revealed in these last times for the sake of people like you, who through him *have come to believe* in God; God's purpose was that you would come to believe and hope in him."

congregation rather than relationships between congregations, still less denominations. But even in the first century dissensions within congregations led to defections and the setting up of new groups (1 Jn 2:19). Schisms begin in local churches. We must recognize quite clearly that there are occasions when the truth of the gospel is threatened, either when basic Christian truths are explicitly denied or when tendencies develop that lead to the denial of Christian truths. Christian loyalty to the gospel may demand, on occasion, the expulsion of heretics from a church or the withdrawal of members from a group that has "gone off the rails." This point needs to be firmly made in the present ecumenical atmosphere where "differences don't matter"—except (I might be allowed to add) when it is the case that a church is judged inadequate because it doesn't have ministers properly ordained by bishops or doesn't acknowledge the pope (requirements which cannot be justified from Scripture).

Yet, when that has been said, the point about love remains essential. There is no getting round it. Love in the church is a priority both because this is the intended nature of the church and because without it the church will not be able to face the world. Hence the importance of the command *love one another deeply,* which is the key phrase in 1:22-25. However, it is fenced in by other points, so that we cannot easily see the basic train of thought that Peter is following. Having introduced the thought as a command in its own right in 1:22, he seems to base it on the fact of the readers' new birth, which he then develops for its own sake in 1:23-25. We should read 2:1 as drawing out the practical consequences of what has just been said, and then 2:2-3 places everything in the context of Christian growth. The idea emerges that growth in Christian love requires the abandonment of various antisocial practices, and only as we do so will we be set free to develop in Christian experience.

Notes: 1:22 The verb "purify" (Gk *hagnizō*) must be distinguished from the verb "sanctify" (Gk *hagiazō*), the associated noun "sanctification" (1:2) and adjective "holy" (1:15-16; 2:5, 9; 3:5), though it belongs to the same realm of ideas. Whereas "holy" refers more to the status of the people of God, "purify" refers to the actual cleansing which they must undergo. For the insight that "holy" is used especially of the new status of Gentiles, I am indebted to Tae Young Kim, "Sanctification and Paul's Gentile Mission" (unpublished M.Th. diss., University of Aberdeen, 1987).

Before the word *heart* the majority of biblical manuscripts insert *clean* or *pure.* If not a

Purity and Love (1:22-25) The section begins by harking back to one of the main characteristics briefly mentioned in the opening description of the ideal nature of Christians. Their calling to salvation takes place through the sanctifying work of the Spirit (1:2). They are to be holy, like God himself (1:15-16). Peter now describes them as people who *have purified* themselves. His use of the perfect tense denotes a state that began in the past and is still the case. We remind ourselves that *holy* is a word used to refer to the people who belong to God and who show the appropriate characteristics.

It has been suggested that, when Paul uses the verb "sanctify," he generally applies it to Gentiles who were formerly not part of God's people (and unclean in the eyes of Jews). Through their faith in Christ they have become part of God's people and are now holy in his eyes (even though non-Christian Jews would still regard them as unholy). They may not yet show all the characteristics of holy people, but the process of becoming like God has begun and will continue.

This same understanding fits the present passage. Peter refers to the conversion of his readers, many of whom were former pagans, saying that through it they have become sanctified. And this is not just their status. The way in which he says that they have purified their souls (compare 1:9) suggests the actual purification of their inner nature, which will issue in new motives, thoughts and actions. This cleansing has taken place through their obedience to the truth (compare 1:2, 14). The *truth* is the gospel, both with its promises and its demands, so that he intends not just an assent to the message but also the commitment to live by it.

Peter's description of his readers implies that they have purified their minds from sinful desires. This act sets them free to love one another genuinely. Peter is here speaking of *philadelphia* (literally, "love of the

---

genuine part of the text, it certainly expresses the intended sense more clearly.

1:23 The *seed* in the metaphor is the semen implanted by the male. The word so translated might also mean "act of sowing or procreation," but this is not so apt in the context. The adjectives *living* and *enduring* are applied elsewhere to God (Dan 6:26), but here they probably qualify *word* (compare Acts 7:38; Heb 4:12).

1:24 Peter also uses *for* to introduce quotations in 1:16 and 2:6, but whereas in these cases he adds the words *it is written* or the like, here he goes straight into the quotation (compare 3:10).

brothers"), which is mutual love between members of a group of people. Usually Christian love is referred to by the word *agapē*, which is care for others *even without reciprocation*. But within the church, if every member shows *agapē* for the others, there will inevitably be response. The members will grow in affection for one another, and strong bonds of unity will develop between them. Peter makes much of this kind of love (2:17; 5:9), but of course this does not mean that he ignores the duty of Christians to show *agapē* to all people. Rather his interest here is the need for right relationships within the Christian congregation. Their love must be *sincere,* free from false motives and pretense.

All that has been said so far represents the ideal, the intended result of sanctification. Now comes the rub. If the ideal is that Christians should love their brothers, then let them *love one another.* Get on and do it. This is a clear and direct command. We must take action without ifs and buts. Peter assumes that Christians can and must love one another.

Think now of the man who sits on the opposite side of the church from you and to whom you rarely speak. Think of the woman in the choir with the cacophonous voice, who ought to have retired voluntarily years ago. Think of that teen-ager with the ghastly hairstyle, who shows an adolescent disdain for an old "square" like you. Do you love them— deeply and from the heart? If not, what excuse can you offer for going against this plain, straightforward command? What excuse can *I* offer?

Peter expresses the command rather forcefully by adding a couple of qualifications. One is that such love should come from a pure heart. This simply repeats the requirement that love be sincere. The other is that love should be exercised *deeply,* that is, strenuously or persistently (compare 4:8).

The motive and ability to obey the commandment to love flow from the new birth and the new life that it opens up. Again Peter takes and applies what he said already earlier in the letter (1:3). He makes it clear that he is thinking of a birth on the spiritual level, which is of higher

---

2:1 In my analysis of the letter, I have treated 2:1-3 as a paragraph within the subsection 1:22—2:3. Its character is problematic. Verse 1 sums up in effect the content of 1:22-25, and verses 2-3 speak about growing up into salvation. By what is little more than a catchword connection, verse 3 leads on to the thought of coming to the Lord in verse 4 and then develops the thought of Christians forming a spiritual temple and a holy, priestly people. Consequently, although a number of scholars place the division between sections at 1:25

worth and quality than physical birth. The spiritual birth is brought about by the word of God, which is understood as the life-giving *seed* planted in the soul. The metaphor is, of course, not to be pressed by asking about the female partner in the act of conception. All that Peter emphasizes is this birth's *eternal* quality, the life of God who is living and enduring and whose Word is therefore also living and enduring. When we hear the Word of God and respond to it with faith, it takes root in our lives and the new birth takes place. But Peter also is saying that the quality of our love must be persistent and enduring precisely because the new life given by God is everlasting.

What Peter has just said he confirms with a quotation from Isaiah 40:6-8. This passage draws a contrast between all human beings (literally, "all flesh") and the words of God. The former resemble grass and have a beauty like the flowers that spring up amid grass. Everyone knows that grass withers and dies, and so do its flowers. So too, human beings will perish, and all that they have to boast of will perish with them. Only the Word of God remains permanently; what he promises will be fulfilled.

What precisely does the quotation confirm? Most probably two things. First, it confirms from Scripture that God's word is *imperishable,* in contrast with human beings. At the same time, of course, it implies that all human beings will pass away as part of the world, which is on its way to destruction. But this is not the primary thought here, merely the background. Second, Peter believes that when Isaiah spoke about the Word of God, he was referring to the gospel that was proclaimed to the readers. In other words, he confirms that the gospel will bring the readers everlasting life.

Purity and Growth (2:1-3) Much current Christian literature is concerned with church growth, the byword for current methods for increasing membership, principally through evangelism. But growth has other dimensions beside the purely numerical one. Two of its most important aspects are the development of spiritual maturity in individual converts

---

and 2:1, it seems more probable to me that 2:1-3 is a transitional section, and that 1:13—2:10 forms a more united section.

The thought of *laying aside* the evil ways of the past is found in Romans 13:12; Ephesians 4:22, 25; Colossians 3:8; Hebrews 12:1 and James 1:21. It was clearly a stock phrase of teachers expounding the character of the Christian life.

This verse has the form of a "vice list," a form of writing found in the New Testament

and the development of the whole fellowship into a loving family. These two aspects come together in this part of the letter.

The picture of bodily growth is frequently used to describe the nature of the Christian life, and it forms the guiding thread of this brief section. Although the point is disputed, it seems most likely that the description of the readers as babies is related to the mention of their new birth in 1:23. The reference would be all the more apt if the original setting of the material in this part was an address given to new members of the church.

First of all, Peter refers with *therefore* to what he said in the previous section: the need for genuine love among the members of the church. Such love can exist only as its opposing motives and practices are purged from the members of the church. Consequently, they are called to *rid* themselves of all that is contrary to love. The verb can be used for taking off one's clothes (Acts 7:58), and it is probable that the metaphor remained alive. In Romans 13:12, a passage that contains similar teaching, Paul's readers are exhorted to lay aside the works of darkness and clothe themselves with the armor of light.

Peter catalogs the love-spoiling vices that Christians must lay aside. *Malice* is the desire to harm other people, which often hides behind apparently good actions (2:16). It reappears in similar contexts in Colossians 3:8 and James 1:21. *Deceit* is the deliberate attempt to mislead other people by telling lies. It is mentioned again as something to be shunned in 3:10, and Christians are reminded that it was conspicuously absent from the behavior of Christ (2:22).

Hypocrisy, like the two following nouns, is in the plural—"every act of" or "every kind of" hypocrisy. This is the kind of deceit in which persons pretend to be different from what they really are, and especially that they are acting from good motives when in reality they are motivated by selfish desire. *Envy,* the longing for what other people have, needs no comment. Finally, *slander* is literally "talking down" other people

---

and in ethical writers in the ancient world generally. Such lists can be used to describe the sins of the pagan world (Rom 1:29-31; Tit 3:3) and also the sins that might carry over into the lives of Christians (Gal 5:19-21; Col 3:5-8). The first two terms are in the singular form, the remaining three in the plural, possibly to give a contrast between general characteristics and individual examples of evil behavior.

("running them down," as we English say). Peter mentions that Christians are treated this way by their enemies (3:16), and so all the more they themselves should avoid slander.

All of these qualities interfere with the activity of love, and from them we can draw up a picture of what love should be. Love does not act from spite; it acts for the good of the other person. Love does not practice cunning or act as a mask for selfish motives; it is honest and open-handed in its dealings. Love does not desire to be better than other people or to destroy other people's reputations; it rejoices in the success of other people and is glad to give them praise and commendation.

The form of the verb used in verse 1 suggests a once-for-all act. It could in fact be saying, "Now that you have rid yourselves," referring to the decisive change of course experienced by the readers at their new birth. Experience, however, suggests that the Christian life is one of repeated saying no to temptation, and that the verb should be taken as an imperative. Thus it stands in parallel with the command in verse 2. Nevertheless, verse 1 still supplies the condition for fulfilling the command in verse 2. Only when we put aside our evil desires will we begin to grow as Christians. Growth is impossible without pruning away the diseased wood.

But growth is also impossible without nourishment. Peter wants to remind his readers that, more than simply receiving spiritual nourishment, they should be ardently longing for it. They should not be like children who eat milk puddings—which they don't really like—because they have been repeatedly told by their mother "It's good for you," but more like children who consume ice cream, with gusto. The newborn child does not interact much with its new environment, but right from the start it ardently desires milk. Christians should show the same eager desire for the spiritual equivalent. They should, to change the metaphor, be hooked on it.

Peter probably continues his metaphor in the word *pure* which can

---

2:2 The use of *milk* as a symbol for spiritual nourishment is found in Judaism and other religions; it would have been immediately familiar to Peter's readers. The author of the Qumran hymns described the "sons of Grace" as opening "their mouth as a ba[be to its mother's breasts] and as a child delighting in the breast of its nurses" (1QH 7:21-22). For the use of *spiritual* see Romans 12:1 and compare the use of *pneumatikos* in 1 Peter 2:5, which is also translated as "spiritual" (NIV).

mean "unadulterated" and refer, for example, to milk that has not been thinned down with water. The idea is that the Christian's nourishment will be free from deceit. There may be a play on words with *deceit* in 2:1.

But what does he mean by *spiritual milk?* The word *spiritual* shows that he is using a metaphor. Literally it means "belonging to the word or reason" (Gk, *logikos* from *logos,* "word"). This may mean "reasonable," as opposed to material, or "metaphorical," as opposed to literal. So the phrase may simply mean "the spiritual equivalent of milk." We are not making much progress! The answer must lie in the word *milk* itself, which was commonly used as a metaphor for religious teaching. It refers elsewhere in the New Testament to elementary teaching, as opposed to the "solid food" given to those who are no longer babies (1 Cor 3:2; Heb 5:12-13). Peter, however, is not thinking of this contrast but simply how Christians all receive nourishment from teaching. The Word of God that brought Christians to birth will continue to sustain them. Kelly holds that the writer could hardly use the word *spiritual* without intending to allude to the *word,* which figures so prominently in 1:22-25 (1969:85).

By receiving such nourishment Christians will grow in spiritual stature. Growth is the next stage toward the goal of *salvation* after birth or after the germination of seed (1 Cor 3:6-7). Does this mean that salvation lies entirely in the future? There is no doubt that "salvation" in the New Testament is primarily something that we receive or experience in the future. Nevertheless, Christians are those who are being saved (Acts 2:47; 1 Cor 1:18; 2 Cor 2:15) and indeed those who have been saved (Eph 2:5, 8; Tit 3:5). If salvation is future in 1:5, it is probably present in 1:9 (but see note). Here Peter is probably thinking of salvation as complete deliverance from sin and its consequences, and then the full growth of love. Toward this goal Christians should be growing.

Peter enjoins his readers to crave spiritual nourishment on the assumption that they have already tasted it and know that it is good—so good that it is worth getting more. They have already proved that the Lord is good by personal experience. There is perhaps more in this

---

2:3 *Now that* is literally "if," with the force "if, as is indeed the case."

The word translated *good* can also mean "delicious" (Lk 5:39), which would fit in with the metaphor of tasting. However, the overwhelming force of its association with *God*

statement than meets the eye.

First of all, verse 3 identifies the nourishment with the Lord rather than with his Word or with teaching about him. This reflects the common Christian belief that in the Word we meet with the Lord himself. It is interesting to compare two very similar verses in the letters of Paul. In Colossians 3:16 he says, "Let the *word* of Christ dwell in you richly." Making essentially the same point in Ephesians 3:17 he says, "That *Christ* may dwell in your hearts." Christ and his Word are equivalent. Similarly, John can write of God, Christ, the Word of God and what Christians have heard as all remaining in the Christian (1 Jn 4:12; Jn 15:4; 1 Jn 2:14; 2:24).

Second, Peter makes this transition from the Word to the Lord because he is in fact backing up his exhortation by a tacit quotation from the Old Testament. Psalm 34:8 says, "Taste and see that the LORD is good." Peter has taken, in effect, the imperative mood from the psalm, used it in verse 2 *(crave)* and then quoted the psalm's actual words as the basis for the command.

Third, although the psalmist was referring to his experience of proving the goodness of God, whom he calls *the Lord,* the next verse in Peter's letter proves that he was identifying Christ as the Lord. Here we have one of the many examples that show how Old Testament texts, originally referring to God, were taken by Christians as references to Christ. In the light of the fact that through Christ they came to know God and that Christ shared the nature of God, Christians felt justified in assuming that what was said about the character of God in the Old Testament also applied to Christ.

Thus Peter aims in this brief section to encourage his readers toward spiritual growth. The condition for growth is the putting away of all that is evil in their relationships with others and the nourishing of themselves by the Word of God. Peter's teaching does not give us the basis for drawing up an orderly set of stages of spiritual growth. Christian growth is organic: progress in one area relates to progress in another.

The Spiritual House and the Chosen People (2:4-10) One of the common criticisms of evangelical Christianity is its weak doctrine of the

coupled with the knowledge that God is good (for example, Lk 6:35; Rom 2:4) suggests that this nuance is probably not alive here. Peter will quote Psalm 34 more fully in 3:10-12.

church. The emphasis lies on the conversion of individuals to personal faith in Christ and little importance is attached to their participation in the church. The idea of the church as an existing "divine society" stretching backward in history and outward to embrace all Christians is passed over in favor of an understanding of the church as separate, voluntary groups of like-minded people. The thought of the church having a priestly character is abhorrent to those who insist that priesthood came to a climax and an end with the sacrifice of Christ on the cross.

No doubt the criticism, as just stated, is exaggerated and not generally applicable to all evangelical Christians. But it would not stick at all if they took to heart the teaching of their supreme authority, the New Testament, and especially of this part of it. In 1 Peter 2 we have one of the strongest expressions of the doctrine of the church, which brings out those points where evangelicals are often felt to be weak. This passage emphasizes: (1) When believers come to Christ, they are at the same time coming into the church; (2) the church has the character of a temple and must fulfill the functions of a temple; (3) the church stands in continuity with the people of God since the time God called Abraham and made him the father of many nations.

At the same time Peter emphasizes the central position of Jesus in the church. In verses 6-8 he develops the thought adumbrated in verse 4 by showing how Christ himself is the keystone of the temple. He refers to the Old Testament Scriptures that lay behind this conception and then argues that people become part of the temple only by being joined by faith to Jesus. Those who reject Jesus will find themselves brought to ruin.

Living Stones (2:4-5) Peter switches rapidly from the metaphor of spiritual nourishment, aided by the statement that the Lord is good, to the concept of coming to him. A further reminiscence from Psalm 34:5 may have helped him also, where he may have understood the verb to

Notes: 2:4 There are various Greek words for *stone.* The one used here *(lithos)* means a piece of stone that has been hewn into shape for use in building as opposed to an irregular lump or a boulder.

2:5 The verb *you . . . are being built* may also (but less probably) be taken as an imperative.

The concept of Christians as a household is regarded as the dominant one by Elliott

mean "come to worship," as it often does in the Septuagint. But this statement is little more than a connection between the previous section and the new thought that now comes to expression.

The basis for the metaphor of stones lies in Psalm 118:22. At some point, presumably under the influence of Jesus' own use of this psalm, Christians saw that the metaphor of a stone helpfully applied to their Lord. They then searched for and discovered the other Old Testament texts that could be taken in the same way. This collection of texts was known to Peter, and he now uses it, identifying Christ as *the living Stone*. The expression's metaphoric character is indicated by the use of the word *living*, which implicitly describes Christ as the risen One.

Peter may have been led to paraphrase Psalm 118:22 by the thought expressed in 2:3 that the readers—as opposed to people outside the church—have tasted that the Lord is good. Outside the church, most people (obviously not all of them, since some have never heard of him) have in fact rejected Christ. Here Peter is employing the picture of a stone that has been dressed or cut and sits ready for incorporation in a building. The builders have passed it over as being unfit for the task. They cannot see that it is the right stone.

But they are wrong, for the stone in question has been approved by the architect. The psalm says the rejected stone is not merely laid as part of the building but as the main foundation stone on which the whole building depends. This, says the psalmist, moving from metaphor to reality, is the Lord's doing. However, instead of repeating the language of the psalm to make this point, Peter quotes Isaiah 28:16, which describes how God lays a foundation stone that is chosen and honored by him. In this way Peter makes an incidental point to his main theme: Whatever the world may think of him, Christ is God's chosen and honored Servant. He will go on to show in a moment how Christ is the prototype for believers, who also are living stones, chosen by God.

(1966:149-59; 1981:169), but the main emphasis of the passage is surely on the house as a temple.

To be a holy priesthood can mean either to be a body of priests or to carry out the holy function of priests. The former interpretation is preferable (in view of the dependence of the phraseology on Ex 19:6), but naturally the priests are there to do priestly service. Possibly Peter is looking forward to the ethical advice that he will give to his readers in the next section of the letter, seeing this as part of the priestly service of believers.

Now comes the main point. Christians who come in faith to Christ will be built into the walls of the building of which Christ is the foundation stone. They form *a spiritual house*. Peter uses a different word here from that in 2:1, but it probably means little more than "metaphorical," spiritual as opposed to material. The *house* can be understood in two ways.

First, a house can be a building in which a family or household lives. This picture is used elsewhere of the church (compare 2 Tim 2:20-21), and it emphasizes the corporate life of Christians under God as their Father, with duties to him and to one another. This thought may well be present here, but it is a background one.

Second, a house can be a temple, in that it is a place where a god dwells. The Jews' temple was the "house of God" not in the sense that he lived there but that he was present there without confinement. Because the temple was the place of God's presence, it was the appropriate place for him to communicate with his people and to receive their gifts, sacrifices and prayers. His presence made it holy—a place to be approached with awe and reverence by people who were themselves holy and permitted to be present. Only the priests were allowed into the central part of the temple in Jerusalem.

These ideas are certainly the main ones in this passage. Peter develops them to make the point that Christians are themselves the temple of God. He does not delve into tricky questions: whether each congregation is a temple or all the congregations collectively and where God's presence is when the members of the congregation are not gathered together. To ask questions of this kind pushes the metaphor too far. The point is rather that, when Christians meet together, they constitute a temple. They have no need of a physical temple at Jerusalem or anywhere else.

Next Peter changes the metaphor slightly, saying that Christians are a *holy priesthood*. They are not only the stones that compose the building but also the priests who work in it. Their task is to offer spiritual sacrifices.

A spiritual sacrifice is not material (or not *only* material) but is an offering of the self (Rom 12:1), expressed in praise, thanksgiving and doing good (Heb 13:15-16; compare Rom 15:16; Phil 2:17; 4:18). Like the material sacrifices in the Old Testament, a spiritual sacrifice must be an offering that God is willing to receive. Not all sacrifices are acceptable to him, particularly those offered from wrong motives or not accompanied by the *right* attitudes toward God and other people (Mic 6:6-8). Spiritual sacrifices acceptable to God are offered *through Jesus Christ.* We fulfill this condition by saying this phrase at the end of our prayers, but the point naturally goes deeper. All our approaches to God come through the mediator whom he has appointed, and they must be acceptable to him in the first place. It is through our knowledge of Christ that we know the character of God and what will be pleasing to him.

It goes without saying that these offerings are not for sin. The sin-offering has been made once and for all by Jesus, and there is a total absence in the New Testament of any language which suggests that Christians share in it. But Christians often forget that sacrifices were prescribed in the Old Testament not only as means of atonement for sin but also as expressions of thanksgiving and communion with God. The grain offering and the fellowship offering, which are described in Leviticus 1—2, were not offered for sin like the burnt offering, the sin offering and the guilt offering. There were appropriate differences in the ritual. If this simple fact were remembered, a lot of confusion about the place of sacrifice in Christian spirituality would be avoided.

Although the prayers spoken at the Lord's Supper were later regarded as an offering, the New Testament itself never regards the Lord's Supper as the offering of a sacrifice—of whatever kind—by the church or the celebrant. Furthermore, to preserve a proper balance, we should note that only rarely is the language of sacrifice applied to what goes on in the church meeting. Christian meetings emphasized hearing the Word of God, responding to it in thanksgiving and prayer, and having fellowship. Temple imagery was not primary in expounding what should happen in a Christian meeting.

Christ as the Stone (2:6-8) One of the biggest objections to belief in God is the fact that so many other people do not believe in him. Christians in the ancient world faced perhaps an even bigger problem: Their religion started as a development within Judaism. Because they shared belief in the same God, the problem of justifying their belief in him to Jews did not arise. In fact, they could even incorporate arguments used by the Jews to convince pagans of the existence of the one true God, Yahweh. The problem lay in the fact that the Jews looked forward to the fulfillment of the Old Testament prophecies of the coming of a deliverer, variously described as a king in the line of David, the Son of man or the Servant of Yahweh. These prophecies were still vital in Jewish faith in the centuries following the Old Testament period. We know of Jewish groups who looked forward eagerly to the coming of this divine deliverer, now referred to by some of them as the Anointed One (Heb, "the Messiah"; Gk, "the Christ").

Christians recognized Jesus as this deliverer and they saw in him the fulfillment of the Old Testament prophecies. But they were quite alone among the Jews in so doing and undoubtedly constituted a minority group within Judaism. Inevitably they faced the questions: Are you alone right? Can it be true that Jesus is the Messiah when the Jewish people as a whole fail to recognize him as such? Is it not rather the case that you are wrong in your identification? Acute questions of this kind must have caused what we today call an identity crisis. Consequently, one important part of Christian apologetics was to provide a convincing explanation as to why so few shared their belief that Jesus was the fulfillment of prophecy about the Messiah.

In these verses Peter tackles this problem. He does so by developing the ideas contained in verse 4 with a fuller citation of the relevant Scripture passages. By quoting these passages he draws a contrast between the Christians who accept Jesus and the non-Christians who reject him and disobey the gospel. He shows that this contrast was foretold in the

---

2:6 *For in Scripture it says* is literally "for it is contained in writing," a unique phrase for introducing a quotation. Selwyn (1947:163) understood the "writing" in question to be a Christian hymn, which consisted of the Old Testament citations with brief added comments. More probably, "in writing" simply means "in the Scripture as a whole" and covers the whole set of quotations. The practice of stringing quotations together and adding comments to explain their significance already existed in Judaism. Two of the documents discovered at Qumran (the *Florilegium* and the *Testimonies* from Cave 4) have this character. That the present three quotations formed a known and more widely used collection of the early church is evidenced in the fact that Psalm 118:22-23 is cited here and in Mark 12:10-11 (compare Mt 21:42; Lk 20:17) and Acts 4:11; Isaiah 8:14 is cited here and in Romans 9:33; Isaiah 28:16 is cited here and in Romans 9:33 and Ephesians 2:20. The wording of the quotations in this passage and in Romans 9:33 show such common divergences from the text of the Greek Old Testament as to demonstrate that Peter and Paul are following a common source.

Capstone is the NIV translation for "head of the corner" and signifies a coping stone at the top of a building. Though there is some evidence for the use of the term with this meaning (2 Kings 25:17), it is probably a mistaken interpretation. The NIV marginal note

Old Testament Scriptures and should not come as a surprise to them. Those who reject Christ will come under judgment, since God has appointed that people stand or fall depending on whether or not they believe in him.

The argument proceeds by quoting and commenting on the three Old Testament texts that Christians believed were referring to Christ as the Stone. The first quotation is from Isaiah 28:16. In this passage God inveighs against Jerusalem's rulers, who have ignored God but think that they are safe from trouble because of their political alliances. God likens himself to a builder who commences a new building in Zion (Jerusalem). He is about to lay a foundation stone, which will be of his own choice and of high quality. The prophet goes on to say that Yahweh's building will be built with justice and righteousness. Anybody who trusts this solid foundation will be like a builder whose edifice stands firmly; he will not suffer the ignominy of seeing his building fall to ruins (like the builder of Jesus' parable in Lk 14:28-30). Isaiah is announcing the need to depend on Yahweh and what he is doing, and to practice righteousness and justice.

Nothing that is said suggests what the stone represents. However, Peter accepts the stone as Christ, an identification that was already current in the church. While it would be wrong to see in the verse a direct prophecy of the coming of Christ, we do have a case of typology: What God was doing in the time of Isaiah is seen as the pattern for what he is now doing

---

cornerstone is right. A stone anchoring the corner of a building (over which a person might stumble) is meant, not a top stone.

2:8 Note that Peter has run his two quotations closely together. It would be better to omit the commas surrounding *and,* and then to punctuate as follows: "The stone the builders rejected has become the cornerstone" and "a stone that causes men to stumble and a rock that makes them fall."

Some commentators take the last part of the verse to mean that unbelievers were destined by God to disbelieve (for example, Selwyn 1947:164-165; Grudem 1988:106-110). This would be a clear statement of the negative side of double predestination, the doctrine that God has foreordained some to life and the rest to destruction. But nothing in the letter supports this view. (Nor, in my view, does anything else in the New Testament. First Thessalonians 5:9 cannot be pressed to yield the meaning "but God has foreordained others to wrath," and Romans 9:22-23 does not say that God has prepared some for inevitable wrath and destruction.) Selwyn and Grudem insist that the rejection of Christ here is not final and irretrievable, but this is a rather desperate expedient. We should be guided rather by 2 Peter 3:9.

in Christ. Moreover, Peter's use implies that God intended what was happening in Isaiah's time to function as a typological anticipation of what he would do later in Christ.

Peter applies the point of this text by commenting, according to NIV, *Now to you who believe, this stone is precious.* Understood in this way Peter simply draws out the point that his readers share God's understanding of Jesus as being of supreme value ("the pearl of great price" in Mt 13:45-46). Whatever the world thinks of Jesus, these believers understand his significance correctly.

But the NIV may not be quite right. The remainder of the section, which indicates how unbelievers will come to ruin, suggests another translation: "For you, therefore, who believe there is honor" (Selwyn 1947:164; Goppelt 1978:149). That is to say, those who believe in Jesus as the Christ will share in the honor that God has bestowed on him. In other words, the word "honor" takes up not the description of the stone as precious but the final clause of the quotation, which says that the believer will not be put to shame (or, positively, will be honored). Here, therefore, we have an anticipation of the description of believers in verses 9-10 as the true people of God.

The decisive thing, then, is whether or not people believe in Christ. If people do not believe, the stone does not, as it were, go away; it remains there. Peter describes its continuing significance for these unbelievers in a twofold way, making use of the two remaining quotations.

The first of these is from Psalm 118:22. The quotation makes two points. First, the stone that was ready for use in the building was rejected by the builders. Second, God nevertheless placed this stone as the capstone (cornerstone, NIV note) of his building. In other words, the builders' verdict on the stone has been rejected. How does this argument of Peter's work? The quotation comes from a psalm about the king going to the temple to give his thanks to God for a military victory. It seems that even among his own people some rejected him and had doubts about his ability; now he had been vindicated by God, who caused his triumph. This verse was quoted by Jesus at the conclusion of the parable

---

2:9 The descriptions of Christians here show that the thought of a "new exodus" is still in Peter's mind. Similar ideas can be found in the Dead Sea Scrolls: The Jewish sect at Qumran believed that God had called them into the desert to make a new beginning. It

of the vineyard, where it makes exactly the same point about the Messiah, the descendant of the king in the psalm. Because Jesus used the psalm about himself, his followers could then build on it: Despite the attitude of the Jewish leaders, Jesus was vindicated by God.

The second quotation, from Isaiah 8:14, reveals the other significance of the stone for unbelievers. In the original context the Lord encourages the prophet not to fear what the people of Israel fear but to fear him (Is 8:12-13, used in 1 Pet 3:14-15), for he will be a sanctuary for the prophet; "but for both houses of Israel he will be a stone that causes men to stumble and a rock that makes them fall."

What is significant, first of all, is that the stone is used as a metaphor for the Lord himself. Presumably, this identification encouraged Christian readers to apply the stone in the other two quotations to a person. Second, the Lord is a stone over which people trip and fall—to their own destruction. This is a metaphorical way of saying that, if people reject Christ, their rejection will be their own undoing. Peter then explains that they stumble as a result of the gospel message, in which Jesus is presented as the Christ. This is what they were destined for; namely, to stumble if they disobey. The stone is set there by God's purpose so that, if people refuse to build on it, it will become the means of their ruin.

We can now see that Peter explains the unbelief of non-Christians as something that was anticipated in the Old Testament, something that should not be surprising. Incidentally, he has reiterated in effect that Christ is the only way of salvation; to reject him is to land oneself in ruin and destruction.

The Chosen People (2:9-10) In the third subsection Peter returns to his readers and proceeds to contrast them with the people who disbelieve the gospel. His concern here is to describe them in language, drawn from the Old Testament, that was originally used to depict Israel as the chosen people of God. He uses five phrases, which are taken from two main passages in the Greek version of the Old Testament. In Exodus 19:6 we read: "You will be my *special people* out of all the nations; for the whole earth is mine; but you will be for me a *royal priesthood* and

---

is impossible to avoid the impression that Peter deliberately says that the contemporary people of Israel are no longer God's people, standing in continuity with his people in Old Testament times, but rather that the church is the true heir of Israel.

a *holy nation.*" In Isaiah 43:20-21 we find: "To give drink to my *chosen people,* my people whom I have made my *special property to declare my praises.*"

The saying in Exodus 19 comes from the passage where Moses is about to receive the Ten Commandments. God makes the preliminary offer to the people of Israel: They can be his people provided they are willing to keep his commandments. The second quotation comes from a passage in Isaiah where God expresses his concern to redeem his people from Babylon and describes how he will provide them with water on their journey home through the desert, just as he did on the way from Egypt to the Promised Land. Now, for a third time, God actively redeems, and Peter identifies his readers as the objects of God's choice and care, the new Israel.

First, they constitute a *chosen nation.* There is a link here with Jesus, who was the chosen stone in verses 4 and 6. This link should not be regarded as pure coincidence. Time and again Peter and the other New Testament writers insist that Christians are what they are in union with Christ and that they share his status and privileges. But the link probably goes deeper. In this part of Isaiah both the Lord's Servant and the people of Israel are chosen by him (compare Is 42:1; 45:4; 49:2), and Israel is spoken of as the Lord's Servant (Is 44:1). There is a sense in which God intended that Israel should be his Servant, but the people refused the role, and it fell to one person to take that role. Now the role that Israel refused in the past is reassigned to the church in union with Christ. Thus, to be a chosen nation is not only an indication of privilege but also a summons to service.

Second, they are a *royal priesthood.* This phrase means that the people constitute a group of priests belonging to a king. Our popular idea of a priest is of a person with the right to offer sacrifice on behalf of others.

The words behind *royal priesthood* can also be taken to mean "a kingdom [and] a priesthood." The original Hebrew has "a kingdom of priests," and this interpretation is found in Revelation 1:6 and 5:10: "a kingdom [and] priests." Elliott (1966) holds that the word translated "royal" is in fact a noun meaning "a king's palace"; this is the meaning of the word in some Jewish sources. Best (1971:107-8) posits the unparalleled sense "a body of kings." But the fact that each of the other three phrases here in 1 Peter consists of a noun with an adjective (or adjectival phrase) speaks in favor of the NIV translation.

In his extended treatment of this passage Elliott (1966) argues that the concept of the corporate priesthood of Israel is drawn from Exodus 19:6 and has nothing to do with the

The basic meaning in the Bible is a person who serves God and has the right of access to him. That is why he is able to bring sacrifices on behalf of people who do not have access to God. Whereas in the Old Testament this privilege was restricted to one of the tribes of Israel, it is now extended to all the members of the new Israel—all members of the church are priests. Again, as we have seen already, there is no atoning sacrifice to be offered in the church. That was done by the high priest, Christ himself. His act is the basis for the doctrine of the "priesthood of all believers," which means that every Christian has in Christ the right of direct access to God without the need for any other mediator. Consequently, too, every Christian has the right to intercede with God on behalf of others.

The practical implications of this are plain. There is no justification here or elsewhere in the New Testament for labeling certain people in the church as "priests." If some Christians are set apart to perform the functions of ministers in the church, they are not to be regarded as priests different in kind from that of all Christians. Above all, there is no biblical justification for holding that the Lord's Supper can be celebrated only by a person who has undergone some kind of ordination to priesthood. The term "priest" should be dropped as a way of designating ministers of the gospel. No matter how much those who use it insist that it does not convey false ideas of priesthood, the term's misleading associations cannot be avoided.

Third, Christians form a *holy people*. This means that they belong to God in a way that other people do not. Above all, it lays on them the obligation to be holy (1:15-16) so that the fact that they are God's people is visible in the quality of their lives.

Fourth, they are God's special property. The Greek phrase here behind *a people belonging to God* conveys the sense that they are a particularly

Levitical priesthood. He suggests that the passage is concerned primarily with the fact that God's people are his elect, who are called to be holy, and he denies any basis in the passage for the doctrine of the priesthood of all believers. His thesis is criticized by Best (1969:270-93), who argues that all members of the church are priests doing priestly service, but that they do so not as individuals but within the corporate existence of the church.

For *a special people* compare Malachi 3:17; Acts 20:28; Ephesians 1:14; and Titus 2:14. The comparison of conversion to coming into the light is common (for example, Acts 26:18; Rom 2:19; 2 Cor 4:6; 1 Thess 5:4-5).

significant and precious possession to him, and therefore the object of his special care.

Finally, Peter brings out the duty and service involved in this position of privilege by stating that God has chosen them to declare his praiseworthy deeds. In the original context in Isaiah 43 the nature of these deeds is not specified. Peter develops the idea in his own words by saying that they are the mighty deeds of the One who has summoned the readers out of darkness into light. Just as God called the people out of Egypt (Hos 11:1) and later out of Babylon, so now he has called people who were living in the darkness of ignorance and sin to be his people and live in the light of his revelation in Christ (compare Eph 5:8). This light should fill God's people with wonder and praise.

Verse 10 forms the last part of Peter's scriptural argument for the standing of his readers as the people of God. It is, in fact, a collection of phrases from Hosea that summarize part of that book's message. The marriage of Hosea and the birth of his children were used as symbols to illustrate God's message to Israel. His daughter was named symbolically Lo-Ruhamah, which means "not pitied," and his son was called Lo-Ammi, which means "not my people." Through these symbolic names God communicated that he would no longer show mercy to the people of Israel or reckon them as his people (Hos 1:6-10).

Nevertheless, Hosea's message was ultimately one of the compassionate love of God, who could not leave Israel to the fate it deserved. The word of God came through him saying: "I will show my love to the one I called 'Not my loved one.' I will say to those called 'Not my people,' 'You are my people,' and they will say, 'You are my God' " (Hos 2:23). This verse was quoted by Paul in Romans 9:25, not as a prophecy of Israel's return to the Lord but of the bringing of the Gentiles into a new relationship with him as his sons (Rom 9:26, quoting Hos 1:10). Evidently this use of the prophecy with reference to the Gentiles was known more widely in the church, and Peter uses it now to express the fact that his readers, Gentiles that they were, were now the people of God and the objects of his mercy.

With this statement the first part of the letter comes to an end. Peter has shown how his readers are God's people, loved by him and called to holiness. They are different from other people in the world, and the rest of Peter's letter will explore the practical consequences of this, especially as they face hostility and even persecution.

Whether or not we are conscious of living in a hostile environment, Peter's teaching is still very relevant to our situation. Its particular importance is that it emphasizes the responsibility that arises out of our position as the people of God: We are obligated to declare the wonderful deeds of God to the world around us. The ignorance of the non-Christian world should be dissipated by the knowledge of God. The message will not be universally accepted, but the obligation is not thereby diminished. Although Peter says little directly to encourage his readers to engage in evangelism and mission, he assumes that they will do so. The point emerges almost casually in reference to wives winning their husbands for the faith (3:1) and to Christians living exemplary lives that will make their opponents ashamed and not being afraid to give a defense of their faith (3:15-16). Moreover, Peter uses the language of evangelism when he writes about the conversion of the readers (1:12, 25; 4:6, 17).

□ Social Conduct (2:11—3:12)

In the first part of his letter Peter has developed a theology of the Christian life based on the perspective that shaped the opening thanksgiving: Christians live a life of hope in this world, solidly rooted in the fact of the resurrection of Jesus and in their own experience of new birth, and joyfully maintained despite the sufferings that they undergo since these are a means of strengthening and proving their faith. From this perspective Christians are seen as the new people of God. They must show their nature as his children by living lives that reflect his holiness. They must have a sincere love for one another within the Christian fellowship. They must act together as the church and in union with Christ to serve God and declare his wonderful deeds.

In all this Peter has focused primarily on Christians—their relations to God and to one another and their spiritual growth and development. The outside world has been mentioned secondarily as the source of tribulation, as the vehicle of an alien lifestyle and as the arena for making known the mighty deeds of God. His readers are regarded as those who have been lifted out of the world into a new community.

But now what about this world outside? How are Christians to live in relation to it? What should their attitude be toward it? The answer to this question will occupy, in two main parts, the remainder of the letter. In the second part (3:13—5:11) Peter will speak more directly of specific crises that might test the faith of believers; his instruction is very much concerned with what to do *if you* should suffer for what is right (3:13). First, however, in this section (2:11—3:12) Peter considers how Christians should live daily in the world. He says basically, "Though we Christians will have to respond to some hostile forces in an unbelieving world, we must live lives of a character that can be recognized for its quality even by non-Christians."

The section has a general introduction setting the pattern of Christian living negatively and positively (2:11-12). Then Peter writes specific teaching dealing with relationships with the state (2:13-17), relationships between slaves and their masters (2:18-20)—followed by a more extended theological motivation (2:21-25)—relationships between wives and husbands (3:1-7), and finally a general admonition to all Christians (3:8-12).

The teaching falls into the kind of pattern which has come to be known as a Household Code. We can trace in various New Testament documents how Christians were taught to behave in their different social relationships (Eph 5:21—6:9; Col 3:18—4:1; Tit 2:1-10). These relationships are largely those of the family—husbands and wives, parents and children, masters and slaves—but also, more broadly, the relationships of citizens to their government and of the old and young. There were, of course, accepted social customs with regard to these relationships, and many of the teachings of Christian writers can also be found in non-Christian authors of the time. This is not surprising. Christians have no monopoly on good ethical teaching, and being a good Christian often includes acting according to the prevailing social standards. The only difference may sometimes be that Christians do so more conscientiously and consistently because they are concerned to keep standards, not just set them up.

Notes: **2:11** *Dear friends* is the signal that a new section of the letter is commencing (compare 4:12).

Sinful desires is literally "fleshly desires." Our bodies are made of flesh, and the word

In applying the teaching given here to our situation we have three problems:

1. If social relationships are different today from what they were in New Testament times, what are the relationships today and how do we frame a Christian morality appropriate to them? For example, nothing is said here about how free employees are related to employers. And nothing is said about the relationships of commercial companies to the communities within which they operate. The structure of marriage is different in some ways. How do we formulate morality for a different set of relationships?

2. Can we take over teaching given for use in relationships that no longer exist or have changed and apply it to our situations? What, for example, can we learn from the ways in which slaves should behave toward their masters?

3. Can we learn anything about the spirit and power of Christian morality? For many modern Christians 1 Peter appears to say nothing about Christian responsibility for social and political change, no sign of a movement to change and improve the world. Even evangelism is assumed rather than openly promoted. How would Peter react to Christians joining in the struggle for liberation in the Third World or expending their energies in the local and national politics of democratic countries? It is no use pretending that these questions do not exist. We are reading 1 Peter to ask what it has to say to us today, and these relationships are part of the situation in which we need to hear the Word of God from Peter.

Strangers in the World (2:11-12) In a well-known passage in *The Pilgrim's Progress,* John Bunyan describes how Christian and Faithful travel through this world to the Celestial City by way of Vanity Fair and are seized because they are not interested in the wares for sale but only in truth. This imagery is derived from passages such as this one. But is it a true representation of what it means to be a Christian in the world?

was appropriately used in the New Testament for the part of us which is weak and responds to temptations, often those of a physical nature (such as gluttony, drunkenness and sexual license) but by no means exclusively so (such as selfishness, violence and hatred). See also 4:1-2.

Does it perhaps present only one side of the truth?

Certainly if Christians are the people of God, this makes them somehow different from other people. This difference must be maintained in their lifestyle. Peter sums it up by describing his readers as *aliens and strangers*. The first part of this description is based on 1:17 where the readers were told to live during the time of their "residence as aliens" in the fear of God. The phrase refers to the way in which a person may temporarily reside in a different country, as, for example, when diplomats are sent to a post for a couple of years in another part of the world. They do not take up permanent residence and change their citizenship; they remain loyal to their own country. Of course they will respect the customs of the country and abide by its laws, but they are not entitled, for example, to vote in its elections or to recognize its rulers as his rulers. They are not expected to accept its religion or its morality.

The second part of the description is repeated from 1:1, where God's people were said to be *strangers in the world*. This word is pretty much a synonym of the first, and, if there is a difference between them, "strangers" expresses more the transient aspect of their stay, while "aliens" expresses more their status as non-citizens. Thus the compound phrase brings out the fact that Christians are in the world for only a temporary period and do not have the status of citizens. They are here today and gone tomorrow. They do not put down firm roots. They belong to another country.

If this is their status, they should not live like the citizens of the world. Peter already told his readers to "put off" sinful habits (2:1). Now he repeats this advice, using the word *abstain* (compare 1 Thess 4:3; 5:22). He also warned them not to conform to the desires of the flesh (1:14). A look back at that verse highlights Peter's picture of his readers as "aliens and strangers" as a pardonable oversimplification.

Normally, the alien is someone who is visiting a country to which he does not in any sense belong. The readers, however, used to belong to the "country" in which they are now aliens. If we want to stretch the

2:12 The principle of conduct expressed here goes back to Matthew 5:16, where Jesus told his followers to let their light shine in such a way that people would see their good works and glorify God. This principle, that Christian conduct must be determined, at least in part, by considering its effects on non-Christians is found throughout the New Testament (1 Cor 10:32; Col 4:5; 1 Thess 4:12; 1 Tim 3:7; 5:14; 6:1; Tit 2:5-10). This is not merely so

metaphor to make it fit, we could think in terms of a person who visits a country and there falls in love with and marries one of the local people. The spouse now adopts the nationality and way of life of the alien and ceases to "belong" to the country where he or she still resides. Clearly a break of this kind, involving a "conversion" that makes people no longer citizens of their own country but resident aliens within it, is all the more difficult to carry through. The temptation to go back to the old way of life must be immensely strong.

In the Christian's case, the temptations must be resisted because of their consequences. The former desires may offer enjoyment and pleasure, but they battle against what Peter calls *your soul*—they are opposed to the "real" interests of the person. The soul has been saved (1:9), but it is threatened by the desires of the flesh, the lower nature, which can pull one's soul down and destroy its life. Just as a musician, for example, can be so enslaved by yielding to sensual desires that his musical faculty is stifled and rendered powerless, so too the Christian can be so diverted from his faith by yielding to temptation that he ceases to be alive toward God.

If the purpose of the instruction in verse 11 seemed to be concerned purely with the personal interests of the readers themselves, verse 12 makes it clear that Peter has a wider horizon. He wants his readers to demonstrate a good way of life among and to the people of the world (see 1:15 note). *Good* will mean conduct that the non-Christians themselves recognize as good, because, as we have emphasized, they are not devoid of moral sense and can recognize and applaud good when they see it. To be sure, standards may differ, but quite a sufficient common ground makes it possible for non-Christians to praise Christians. (Equally, Christians will be able to recognize and approve the good deeds of non-Christians, no matter how much they insist on their total depravity so far as earning salvation is concerned.)

To live in this way is of particular importance because the standing temptation to non-Christians is to "run down" Christians as evildoers and

---

that non-Christians might be left without excuse at the last judgment or recognize that Christians are good people and stop troubling them. Christians are to behave well so that the pagans themselves will come to glorify God. Glorifying God is an activity of believers or at least of people on the way to belief. Hence "to glorify God" may have been a synonym for "to be converted."

perhaps even to accuse them of being criminals (3:16; compare 2:1). The early history of the church shows that Peter was not romancing. Stories circulated that Christians engaged in incest and even cannibalism at their church meetings. Even Tacitus, who was a responsible Roman historian, commented that they were "loathed for their vices."

Accusations of this kind are psychologically explicable but extraordinarily hard to counter. Peter proposes the simple solution that Christians must overcome the slander by living lives of such exemplary goodness that other people will recognize the false accusations. He hopes that they will end up glorifying God for what they now recognize to be good deeds.

This will happen *on the day he visits us,* an Old Testament phrase that may refer to the day of judgment (Is 10:3). However, it may also refer to the day when God shows his mercy to people. So we cannot be certain that Peter means simply that they will recognize Christians as good people after all on the day when they are judged by God. More likely Peter means that seeing and recognizing good deeds will lead some of those Gentiles who formerly slandered them to praise God instead. Such a change of heart can surely include the possibility of a genuine conversion to Christianity (so Grudem 1988:116-17 but compare Balch 1981:87).

From all this we see that Christians are strangers in the world insofar as it is sinful. Yet citizens of the world recognize a basic goodness, and Christians should live by the good standards of the world. In this way they may hope to lead others to recognize and submit to the claims of God.

Peter has adopted a very positive attitude to the situation of the Christian in a hostile environment. His general introduction to this part of the letter is concerned with positively doing good that will be recognized as such in the community and that can play a part in leading other people to know and praise God. This is far from being a world-denying attitude.

2:13 *King* here probably signifies the Roman emperor, because at this time all the specific areas in which Peter's readers lived (1:1) were administered by provincial governors appointed from Rome. The Greek term admittedly means "king" and is used as the equivalent of Latin *rex.* Although the Romans themselves disliked the term, Greek speakers used it as the most appropriate. The word translated *authority* is literally "creation." This may refer to a created object or to the "creation or founding" of something. Most commentators adopt the former sense and understand it to refer to created entities in accordance with the

It requires of Christians that they actively involve themselves in the life of the world rather than that they retreat from it.

Therefore, although Peter says nothing directly about social and political change, we can surely claim that his stress on doing good in society should not be confined to personal, individual acts of kindness but should include participation in communal efforts to change and improve the structures of society. Christians should be in the vanguard of social reform.

The Ruling Authorities (2:13-17) Teaching about the Christian and the state is not too plentiful in the New Testament. It is basically confined to Mark 12:14-17 (and parallels), Romans 13:1-7, 1 Timothy 2:1-3, Titus 3:1-3 and the present passage. In the epistles the teaching is repeatedly about the necessity to submit to the state authorities, whose task is to preserve law and order. Christians are to show themselves as model citizens by not going against the law but rather doing what will commend themselves to the authorities.

In the light of the preceding paragraph we can see the practical necessity of this. Christians are often the target of attacks that take advantage of any way in which they fall below the perceived or ideal standards of the community. Therefore they must disarm all such criticism by going out of their way to be law-abiding and to fulfill the responsibilities of their various stations in life. But the motivation goes deeper than mere desire for self-preservation; it has a theological basis: Obedience must be rendered for the sake of the Lord, who has appointed the authorities to carry out his will.

The crucial term which recurs throughout teaching passages like the present one is *submit yourselves* (2:18; 3:1, 5, 22; 5:5). It is applied to slaves in relation to masters, wives in relation to husbands, the angels and other powers in relation to Christ, and young people in relation to

position which God has given them. Thus the position of a ruler is something that God has appointed. Neugebauer (1979:85-86) suggests that here Peter contests the growing cult of the emperor as a divine being, saying instead that obedience is due to created beings and not to persons who usurp God's place. Selwyn (1947:172) adopts the alternative meaning and takes it to refer to "every fundamental social institution" set up among mankind, including the state, the household and the family. On this reading verse 13 becomes a heading for the whole section of 2:13—3:12.

older people. "Submitting" literally means "placing oneself below another person," out of a respect that is expressed in obedience appropriate to the relationship. It may be compulsory or voluntary.

Obedience is to be rendered to *every authority instituted among men.* This includes political authorities at all levels, and Peter gives as examples the king and his subordinate officials or governors.

Obedience is to be rendered *for the Lord's sake.* Usually "the Lord" means Jesus, and this is likely here. There may be an implicit allusion to Jesus' specific command that his followers are to render to the Roman emperor what is due to him. But certainly the thought is that, as the servants of the Lord, they must honor him in the world by behaving in the appropriate ways.

Peter provides further justification by describing governors as being appointed both to punish offenders and commend those who do good. Here Peter speaks the language of the Greco-Roman world, which commended "doing good." The implication is that Christians are not only to avoid breaking the law but also to do what will win recognition as good deeds. At the extreme, rich citizens were expected to provide lavishly for the needs of the community. The benefactor was a recognized figure. Here is an implicit justification for a positive contribution to the life of the community according to a person's ability.

Peter thus underscores the point already made in 2:12 that, if Christians do positive good in society, they will demonstrate that the slander against them is baseless. The *ignorant talk of foolish men,* who have not bothered to find out the facts, is readily believed (everybody enjoys scandal), and a concerted effort of good actions is required to disprove them. What starts off, then, as apparently a lesson in political passivity culminates in an injunction to take an active role in society. Christians are to be strangers and pilgrims so far as the sinful way of life of the

---

2:16 *As a cover-up for evil* needs some careful unpacking. The underlying Greek word means a "cloak" or "covering." The translations vary as to how they understand it. The NIV, along with many other versions, understands the phrase to refer to Christians using their freedom as a means of hiding their evil behavior. But how can freedom hide evil? Only perhaps in the sense that a deed which other people criticize rightly as evildoing is now alleged not to be an evil deed but the exercise of lawful freedom. For example, a person who commits an act branded by society as adultery may protest that it is not adultery but

world is concerned; but where it is a case of doing good, they are to take an active part.

In verse 16 an interesting qualification is added. Christians are to be subject to the emperor and the governors as free people. They are God's slaves and as such are free from obligation to anybody else. He has redeemed them from slavery to any other power (1:18). Nevertheless, two qualifications are involved. First, as Peter states, their freedom is freedom to do what is right. Redemption here is understood as a change of master rather than as the conferring of absolute liberty (1 Cor 7:22-23; Gal 5:13). God's slaves are slaves to doing good. They are not to claim that their freedom allows them to do wrong and to disobey human commands. Second, their freedom does not permit them to disobey God, whose slaves they are, nor by extension those whom God has appointed to act as lawful authorities.

Finally, the implications of living as God's slaves are spelled out in a straightforward conclusion (v. 17).

First, Christians are to honor everybody, no matter what their position. This appears to be a unique command in the New Testament because it is not confined to honoring fellow-Christians. Indeed the context makes it clear that Peter means people outside the church. They are not to be despised because they are not believers, nor hated because they are persecutors, nor treated with contempt because they are of lower rank or status, but treated with honor. It inevitably follows that people are not to be regarded as second-class citizens because they are of a different race or color.

Second, they are to love the community of brothers, the Christian church. This is hardly a restriction of love to the believing community. Peter would not have quarreled with Jesus' command to love one's enemies.

---

the exercise of sexual freedom. The implication is that the person knows all the time that he is really doing wrong but pretends that it is really acting in freedom. Understood in this way the phrase almost means an "excuse" for evil (RSV, "pretext"). The sense then is "as a cover-up for the evil motivation of their acts by alleging that they are done in the exercise of freedom."

2:17 The NIV obscures the fact that the same Greek word is used for *show proper respect* and for *honor*. Again, the NIV punctuation after the first clause—a colon—is misleading; the first imperative is not a summary of what follows.

Third, they are to fear God. This time the command is restrictive; they are not to fear anybody else. "Fear him you saints, and you will then have nothing else to fear." Those who fear God are delivered from fear of other people, because they know that he will keep them in safety.

Fourth, they are to honor the king. Not to fear him, because that is reserved for God. Does this mean that he is to be treated just like *everyone* earlier in the verse? Some take it to mean that the king should be given the honor appropriate to his position. But does that mean a slave should be given merely the honor due to his position (which isn't very much)? It is unlikely that Peter meant his teaching to be taken quite so literally.

We should be impressed by the nature of the teaching in these verses. Peter exhibits a firm insistence here on the positive, outgoing duty of Christians as members in society, involving honoring and respecting everybody. He exhorts Christians to live in the world and as part of the world, not simply as passing strangers.

Some modern readers will dislike the idea of political submissiveness. They may need to be reminded that any government is impossible without respect for rulers. What Peter says about freedom is not a license for doing wrong. But with the stress on doing good and on the responsibility of rulers to act justly, there may well be the implication that Christians may need to fulfill their political responsibility by acting against the government when it deserves criticism in the name of justice and goodness.

Difficulties arise when dissent seems to require violent action or at least cooperation with other groups whose methods Christians would not always approve. If it is agreed that a police force must have the right to use force and even to resort to arms against violent criminals, should private persons have the same right over against a police force or government that uses violence to oppress the people? Such a path too often can lead to the escalation of violence, to a thirst for revenge and to injuries to the innocent. Only, it would seem, if these risks can be

Notes: 2:18 On slavery in the ancient world see Bartchy (1973) and Judge (1980). For further teaching on slaves in the New Testament see 1 Corinthians 7:21; Ephesians 6:5-8; Colossians 3:22-25; 1 Timothy 6:1-2; and Titus 2:9-10.

Peter uses the word *oiketēs* here instead of *doulos* (used in 2:16 of all Christians); it refers specifically to a household slave.

avoided, should this path be taken.

Slaves and Their Masters (2:18-20) Modern translations of the Bible generally do not put the word "servant" for the Greek word *doulos*, although the latter can refer to a slave *or* servant. Using *slave* preserves the distance between the biblical world and our own, reminding us that the teaching in this section was intended for people in a relationship no longer a part of our social set-up. We are concerned with employee-employer relations, trade unions, restrictive practices, closed shops, lockouts, government-imposed wage settlements and so on. Nevertheless, there are similarities between the employee and the slave, and we can still profit from what Peter had to say.

The conditions of slaves in the ancient world varied enormously. The situation presupposed here is largely that of domestic slaves working in large houses, estates and farms. But there were also large numbers of public slaves, and, in Asia Minor, some large temple estates whose workers were more like serfs. People were enslaved for various reasons: being the children of slaves, being prisoners of war or falling into debt. Their conditions of service also varied.

The general tendency in New Testament times was toward improving the lot of slaves. Manumission was possible if a slave could raise sufficient money from his earnings to secure redemption or could make a contract to continue to serve his former master as a free person. Nevertheless, slaves had no legal position, and a recalcitrant slave was very much at the mercy of his owner. Appalling riots among the vast armies of slaves who worked on gigantic farms in Italy were put down with immense cruelty.

Unlike Paul, who taught mainly slaves with Christian masters, Peter is concerned here with slaves working in the homes of pagan masters. In a Christian household the close contact of slaves and masters could lead to brotherhood (which, however, a slave might misuse, as in 1 Tim 6:2). In a pagan household this familiarity increased the possibilities of fric-

Although the NIV translation *with all respect* suggests that they are to respect their masters (which is a true sentiment; see Eph 6:5), the Greek phrase (literally, "with fear") more probably refers to the fear *of God* (as in v. 17 and so explicitly in Col 3:22). Because they fear and obey God, they should perform the duties appropriate to the relationship in which they have been put.

tion, especially if Christian slaves, who now believed themselves spiritually equal to their masters, tried to force their position. Whatever their situation, Christian slaves should fulfill their obligation to be subject to their masters. Whether their masters are gentle or perverse is not the point; the relationship demands obedience.

This advice cannot have been easy to accept. Slaves could well suffer at the hands of their masters. Peter calls it *unjust* suffering. This contrasts with the view of many people who would have argued (like Aristotle) that, strictly speaking, one couldn't be unjust to a slave because slaves were not persons, but chattels and workhorses. This view was not universal (the Stoics repudiated it, for example). And naturally Christians recognized that slaves were people.

Even without Christian theology to back up the idea, common sense would suggest that on occasions slaves did suffer unjustly. Such suffering dehumanizes people. Treat a person like an animal, and there is a real danger that he will become one.

Nevertheless, Peter says, it is possible to bear unjust suffering in a different way. When a person puts up with suffering *because he is conscious of God, this is commendable.* These two phrases are difficult to understand even if their general sense is clear. The NIV text interprets them to mean that if slaves bear suffering because they are conscious of

2:19 The phrase *because he is conscious of God,* which literally translates "because of conscience of God," can be interpreted in various ways. The word "conscience" is normally used in Greek to refer to that aspect of the mind or personality that passes judgment on past conduct. The conscience functions by condemning actions that are morally wrong in accordance with its own standards of morality. A "good conscience" does not utter a negative verdict on past actions. However, the noun is less commonly used in the context of commendation; the word connotes negative reactions or the absence of them. Again, although conscience typically operates on what a person has done, it can also function as the mental faculty that gives a verdict in advance on what a person is about to do. We all know what it is to hold back from an action because we know inwardly that it would be wrong. We feel uncomfortable at the thought. More broadly, the conscience can judge the whole of our conduct in relationship to God and to other people. When Peter talks about having a *clear conscience* in 3:16 and 21, he means that the person concerned is not conscious of having done wrong.

But what is a *conscience of God?* The oddity of the phrase leads many commentators to suppose that the word cannot have its normal sense but simply means "awareness," perhaps as shared with other Christians. Kelly paraphrases "because of the knowledge of God which he and his fellow Christians share as members of God's holy people" (1969:117). This is how NIV takes the phrase. But the word in its technical sense can mean that a person should act in a particular way because it is prescribed by a conscience which is directed toward

God's will and prepared to obey it, then they find favor with God. According to Goppelt, if people bear suffering because their consciences, determined by the desire to obey God, tell them that they are acting rightly, then their suffering will become for them an experience of God's grace.

Peter confirms this point by an appeal to the moral and spiritual sense of the readers. It stands to reason that if slaves receive a physical beating or lashing because they have committed some misdemeanor or crime, there is no particular credit to them for it, even if they bear it patiently. (There may, of course, be a certain credit for taking one's penalty patiently and acknowledging that it is well deserved in comparison with trying to evade it or protesting loudly against it, but Peter is not thinking of this.) However, if a slave endures suffering that is undeserved—indeed, punishment actually inflicted for doing good—then this is a different story. This is commendable in the sight of God.

If we now try to "translate" this teaching into modern terms, the following points can be made:

1. In all social relationships our conduct should spring out of our reverence for God and our desire to do his will. The fundamental question must always be: What does God want me to do? What Peter says here is a principle of general application.

God. With this interpretation "conscience" is almost equivalent to "faith" (compare 1 Cor 8:10-12 with Rom 14:1), and implies a faith in God that determines a person's actions (Goppelt 1978:195-96).

It is commendable is literally "it is grace," a phrase which can be understood in various ways: (1) it is a gracious act; (2) it is an act deserving gratitude; (3) it is an act that brings [God's] favor; (4) it is an act that leads to an experience of grace. The phrase is repeated in verse 20: *this is commendable before God.* In between these two mentions stands the question *How is it to your credit* [literally, "what glory is it"] *if you receive a beating for doing wrong?* The parallel, the intervening question and also the similar use of the word in Luke 6:32-33 give strong support to the third view, which the NIV adopts. Goppelt (1978:197) defends the fourth view above: through unjust suffering, patiently borne, Christians experience more deeply the grace of God. Through grace we receive the strength to bear it and in suffering it we are the more conscious of this "grace to help in time of need." This is theologically attractive but hard to justify exegetically.

The actual verb meaning "suffer" appears for the first time in the letter in this verse and recurs in 2:20, 21, 23; 3:14, 17, 18; 4:1, 15, 19; 5:10. Twelve of the forty-one New Testament occurrences of the verb come in this brief letter, together with four of the sixteen occurrences of the noun form (1:11; 4:13; 5:1, 9). These figures indicate clearly that suffering is a major theme in 1 Peter.

2. Our conduct in all our relationships should fulfill the obligations imposed by the relationship. A contract to work for some other person or body must be fulfilled conscientiously. To enter into a relationship is to accept obligations. The problem arises with relationships that are imposed on us—relationships as diverse as those of children born to their parents and of people who fall under the control of an enemy power. To what extent do these relationships impose binding obligations upon us? How do we know that it is God's will that we are placed in them?

3. Our conduct in the relationship must be determined by the relationship and not by personal considerations regarding the character of an employer.

4. Disregarding our obligations brings no credit to the gospel, even if we are prepared to pay the price without complaining.

5. If we do suffer unjustly, our acceptance of this without retaliation is commendable (as verse 23 will make clear). Clearly this covers all situations of persecution. These points, given by Peter in a specific context, are surely of universal validity. However, he says nothing about Christians taking action either to get rid of slavery and other practices that treat people as less than human or to withstand injustice. A Christian conscience today may argue that it is our duty to act in such situations. Isn't Peter's advice an acquiescence to an evil structure in society or to the commission of crime and injustice?

A clue to Peter's "answer" might be found if we consider further what is meant by *bearing suffering*. This phrase probably means "bearing it *without retaliation.*" One can take action against injustice and unjust structures in society without engaging in personal retaliation. Whether Peter would have taken this step is not clear. Or is it? If Christians condemned sin in their preaching and by their way of life (2:12; 3:16), was not this one way of taking action against injustice? To be sure, not all types of action for social reconstruction are necessarily legitimate for the Christian, but the fundamental Christian responsibility to work for social justice is a legitimate and necessary development of biblical teaching.

Notes: 2:21 Peter writes *suffered* rather than simply "died" (although some manuscripts have the latter; compare 3:18 for the same textual problem). The verb throbs like a repeated

The Basis for Christian Living (2:21-25) In many ways this paragraph, which stands virtually at the center of the letter, is its theological center. Sandwiched into the section on how people are to behave in their different relationships, it may give the impression of being a digression, a mere back-up for the teaching given to slaves in the preceding verses. But in fact what it says goes far beyond the immediate problem and provides the basis for all Christian behavior.

Peter starts off by motivating Christian slaves to proper conduct with reference to the example of Jesus, who put up with unjust suffering just as they are called to do. But right from the opening phrase it is apparent that Peter is presenting far more than an example. He briefly tells the story of the Christ who *suffered for you* and develops a doctrine of Christ's death that shows how Christians can be transformed to live for righteousness.

It would be almost a sin not to quote here the classic words of James Denney (or not to encourage a reading of his whole book):

It is as though the apostle could not turn his eyes to the cross for a moment without being fascinated and held by it. He saw more in it habitually, and he saw far more in it now than was needed to point his exhortation to the wronged slaves. It is not *their* interest in it, as the supreme example of suffering innocence and patience, but the interest of all sinners in it as the only source of redemption by which he is ultimately inspired. (1951:57)

Here, then, is the fundamental theological statement of the basis of the Christian life in terms of the death of Jesus. It becomes obvious, as we read through the paragraph, that Christ cannot be an example of suffering for us to follow unless he is first of all the Savior whose sufferings were endured on our behalf.

To the surprise of some commentators Peter does not summarize the historical facts surrounding the death of Jesus, which would depict him as an example of patient suffering. These were readily remembered by eyewitnesses like himself and recorded in the Gospels. Instead Peter prefers to describe the sufferings of Jesus in terms drawn from the por-

---

refrain throughout the letter from 2:19 onwards (see note) and colors everything that is said. The same verb is used in the Gospels to refer to the dying of Jesus and all the associated suffering.

trait of the Suffering Servant of Yahweh in Isaiah 53. As such he is not concerned simply to present the facts of Jesus' suffering but rather to explain its theological significance: Jesus suffers as the Servant of Yahweh and fulfills his destiny to bear the sins of others and so bring them to God.

First Peter starts with the calling of the readers. They are people who have been called by God out of darkness into light (2:9) to inherit promised blessings (3:9) that culminate in eternal glory (5:10). But their calling to be the people of God, with all its attendant blessings, involves them now in suffering (1:6). Therefore, it is important to observe that in the present section Peter is not telling his readers that they are called to suffering. As he has already made clear, unjust suffering is not necessarily the inevitable lot of each individual reader. Instead he says that if they suffer, they must bear it patiently. When he says that they were called *to this,* he means that they were called to the *patient* endurance of suffering.

But why must they bear it patiently? Peter gives not a motive for bearing suffering—such as, you ought to bear suffering in order that you may follow the example of Christ—but a reason to endure: you ought to bear suffering because Christ suffered patiently for you and set the example. Let's explore his twofold reason:

1. Basically Christians must suffer patiently because Christ suffered in this way for them. Right at the outset Peter comments that Christ suffered *for you.* His death was on behalf of other people and for their benefit. His self-sacrifice with its attendant suffering saves them from their sins and from divine judgment, but this does not free them from the necessity of enduring suffering. Christ has called them to a new way of life which involves patient suffering like his. As his followers, they must share his lot.

2. Peter says Christ left them an *example.* This word in Greek conjures up pictures of a teacher writing down the letters of the alphabet so that children who are learning to write can copy them, or of an architect drawing a building so that the builders can copy it. Jesus modeled patient suffering for Christians to follow. The way in which he endured his

---

2:22 The Hebrew of Isaiah 53:9 has "violence"; the Septuagint reads "lawlessness"; Peter has put more generally *sin,* possibly to gain a contrast with *sins* in verse 24. Christ suffered not because he had sinned but because he was bearing the sins of others.

2:23 Although there is no direct reference to the text of Isaiah 53, the thought "he did not open his mouth" in 53:7 may lie behind the present verse. See also Romans 12:19 for similar teaching.

suffering is the binding pattern that those who have been saved by the death of Christ must follow.

Put otherwise, Christ has made a path for them, and they must go the way that he has already gone. There may be many possible ways to the summit of a mountain. But the guide chooses the particular path which he himself takes, and his followers must go the same way. But, whereas the mountain-guide may be primarily concerned with safety, Christ is concerned with how his followers live. Just as during his earthly life he called various people to be his disciples and said, "Follow me," so now as the crucified and risen Lord he still calls people to follow him in a path that leads, like his, through possible suffering, and they must follow this path in the same kind of way he did.

Peter uses five phrases to describe the pattern of patient endurance Christ displayed on the cross. The first two are taken from Isaiah 53:9: "though he had done no violence, nor was any deceit in his mouth." These phrases emphasize that the death of Christ was an act of injustice; he had done nothing to deserve it. They implicitly remind Peter's readers that there is no credit in bearing suffering that is the due recompense for evildoing (2:20) and that deceit is one form of evildoing (2:1). The pattern of Christ's life underlies teaching elsewhere in the letter on how Christians ought to live at all times.

The third and fourth phrases form a pair. This time, however, the language of Isaiah 53 is forsaken for a reference to Christ's actual conduct as recorded in the Gospels. Christ was the object of verbal abuse, but he did not reply in kind nor did he make threats to his executioners. In these respects his conduct was different from many celebrated Jewish martyrs, who told their executioners in plain terms the fate that awaited them at the hands of God. Moreover, Jesus taught his hearers not merely to refrain from counter-abuse and threats, but to "bless those who curse [them], pray for those who mistreat [them]" (Lk 6:28). This teaching is echoed later in 1 Peter 3:9.

For the Jewish martyrs see 2 Maccabees 7:17, 19, 31-38; and 4 Maccabees 10:11. We must emphasize, however, that other Jewish sources present a different picture of how martyrs should behave. Jesus was not unique in his attitude.

Clearly *him who judges* is a reference to God, although some scribes, who misunderstood the reference to be to Pilate, found it necessary to alter the text to read "to him who judges *unjustly*"!

The fifth phrase states that instead of attacking his opponents Christ was content to commit his case to the one who judges justly. He left his destiny in the hands of God and obeyed the principle that a person should not seek vengeance but rather leave the judgment of one's opponents to God. The point of this is obviously not that Christians should refrain from defending themselves in a court of law when it is necessary to do so, but rather that they should not seek revenge on people who injure them (Rom 12:19-21).

Peter then continues to describe the sufferings of Jesus in language drawn from Isaiah 53:4. We notice, first, that Peter stresses the reality of the death of Jesus. The words *himself* and *in his body* (compare 3:18) underline this fact. Nothing else in the letter indicates that Peter was attacking any sort of heretical view that contested the physical reality of the Incarnation or bodily death of Jesus. More likely, Peter simply drives home the fact that Jesus really suffered physically. *On the cross* may well allude to the fact that Christ shared the kind of execution which was normally reserved for slaves and rebels.

Second, Peter reiterates an idea from verse 21 that reminds his readers that Jesus' suffering was more than an example to be followed. It had a purpose: Christ bore our sins. The fact that the words *our sins* are placed first and emphatically in the Greek sentence indicates Peter's deliberate intent to go far beyond presenting Christ as an example. He teaches that Christ bore our sins in the sense that he took their consequences upon himself and, by his sacrificial death, atoned for them. " 'Bearing sins' means taking the blame for sins, accepting the punishment due for them, and so securing their putting away" (Kelly 1969:123).

The purpose of this sacrificial act, however, is not simply that we should be set free from the consequences of our sins. Peter sees it as an act which is meant to set us free from sin itself—*so that we might die to sins and live for righteousness.* Paul expresses the point by saying that we share in

---

2:24 In Isaiah 53:4 (Heb text) the prophet, speaking on behalf of the people, says, "he took up our *infirmities* and carried our sorrows." In the Gk version used by Peter this was expressed as "he carries our *sins* and suffers pain for us." These two lines of understanding both appear in the New Testament. Matthew cites this verse in the form "He took up our infirmities and carried our diseases" (8:17) and sees it fulfilled in the healings performed by Jesus. Peter, however, links Isaiah 53:4 with 53:12 ("he bore the sin of many") and sees it as a reference to the death of Christ for our sins. In a rather bold metaphor, Christ takes

the death of Jesus as a death to sin (Rom 6:11, 13, 18; Gal 2:19). He pictures people who by death leave one world and by resurrection enter into a new one. They are separated off from acts of sin to live righteously. Peter develops this point further by two metaphors again taken from Isaiah 53. The first is that of healing. The readers are people who were suffering from illness but are now restored to health. Illness signifies weakness and inability to resist temptation. The person who is healed is not only delivered from illness—and possible death—but has the strength to overcome temptation and to do good. The healing is brought about by the wounds of Jesus. In Isaiah 53:5 the Servant of Yahweh has been wounded and abused because of the sins of the people; by his bearing the lash they are healed.

The prophet started with the Servant suffering wounds as part of his self-sacrifice and submission to innocent suffering and then developed the metaphor by drawing a contrast: as his body was wounded, so the people are healed. Here, then, we have the basis for thinking of salvation in terms of healing, a metaphor that is not developed as much in the New Testament as we might have expected, although it is hard to believe that the healing stories in the Gospels were not used as illustrations of spiritual healing (compare Mk 2:1-10; Jn 9).

The second picture is the familiar one of sheep who wander from the rest of the flock and are in mortal danger of falling off cliffs or being ravaged by wild animals or stolen by thieves. Peter takes this pastoral picture provided in Isaiah 53:6 further in two respects. First, he speaks of the sheep turning back to the shepherd. The verb is elsewhere trans-lated "be converted" (Mk 4:12; Acts 3:19; 1 Thess 1:9) and pictures the beginning of the Christian life in terms of people going in one direction, namely, along the path of sin that leads to destruction, and then doing an about-face to come back to God on the way that leads to life. Peter identifies the shepherd as Christ (5:4; Jn 10:11, 14; Heb 13:20). This

---

on himself the wounds that are the painful expression of our "illness" and by bearing them for us frees us from the "illness."

The verb translated bore (Gk anapherō) is a different word from that used for bears up under in 2:19-20 and means more "to carry." It does not mean that Christ carried our sins onto the cross or that he placed them on an altar. Rather he "took away" our sins by atoning for them in that he bore their consequences in his death on the cross. The thought is probably the same as that expressed in John 1:29 and 1 John 3:5, where we read that Jesus

picture of Christ was evidently a familiar one in the early church.

Second, Peter develops the sheep metaphor by adding the idea of Christ as the *Overseer* of the souls of the readers. This same word elsewhere denotes church leaders and is traditionally translated "bishop," a person who exercises supervision and care over others. It is interesting how Peter takes over a word which originally applied to church leaders and applies it here to Jesus. (Later, in 5:2, he takes over the word "shepherd," which probably was used first with reference to Jesus, and applies it to church leaders.) Christ is thus the Chief Shepherd (5:4) and the (Chief) Overseer of the people of God.

Peter's point in this verse is that when people are converted they come under Jesus' care; the thought of Jesus as an example of patient suffering has retreated into the background. Peter has moved from that to thoughts of Christ as the Suffering Servant who takes away the sins of the readers and as the Shepherd who now cares for them in all their needs. Through Christ the care of God for his people is made known (see 5:7).

So we see that teaching originally motivated by the phenomenon of Christian slaves facing unjust treatment has fundamental importance for every Christian. And although Peter expresses it in the form of a description of what Jesus has done for his readers, his teaching is, in effect, a presentation of the gospel—a statement of what Christ has done for sinners and what is involved in conversion. It speaks to those who are conscious that their lives are dominated by sin and promises release from sin. It contains the offer of forgiveness and the possibility of a new life.

Peter's teaching also clearly states what is involved in following Christ. The pattern that must be followed is his refusal to retaliate when he was attacked. Insofar as violence and war are forms of retaliation, they are here forbidden to the Christian. If war can be defended, it can only be as the lawful use of force to restrain evildoers and not as a means of retaliation.

---

is "the Lamb of God who takes away [Gk *airō*] the sin of the world" and that "he appeared so that he might take away our sins." In the Johannine passages the verb means "to remove or forgive sin" (as in 1 Sam 15:25; 25:28) or to atone for it by bearing its consequences (Num 14:33-34; Is 53:11-12; Ezek 18:19-20). The sacrificial reference is clear from the use of "lamb." The fact that Peter has already spoken of Jesus as a lamb in 1:19 encourages us to interpret the present verse in terms of sacrifice, but in any case the language of Isaiah 53 itself is definitely sacrificial.

The verb *apoginomai* for *die to sins* occurs only here in the New Testament. It means

Of course, people will try to get round this command. They will question how far teaching given by Peter for individuals suffering unjustly, especially for being Christians (4:16), can be extended to apply to individuals or communities suffering injustice for other reasons. On a broader level, the problem is that often there is no international law enforcing punitive action that can be taken against criminal acts by nations. Is there a difference between what one may do with respect to oneself and on behalf of other people who are the victims of injustice?

Some will blur the line between retaliation and deterrence. They argue that taking an eye for an eye will deter your opponent from trying to take another eye in the future. This procedure often works; that is its justification.

Clearly these problems must be borne in mind in applying Peter's teaching. We may reply:

1. Peter's teaching about how slaves should behave is derived from his general understanding of how Christians should react to injustice (3:9, 16; 4:14-19). He drew no distinction between the reactions of Christians as individuals and as a community.

2. Where a framework of law exists, Christians should act within it. Where there is no such framework, Christians should surely behave as those who are under God's laws. When the writer of Judges comments, "In those days Israel had no king; everyone did as he saw fit" (Judg 17:6), the implication is surely that wrong behavior was still wrong behavior even if there was no king to check it.

3. Peter's teaching is about retaliation when you are being persecuted and not about the securing of justice for the oppressed. There is a distinction between the two. Nothing that is said here runs contrary to the expression of Christian love in seeking the rights of the oppressed. But this duty lies outside the horizon of Peter's concern here (that per-

---

"to be away from" or "to have no part in something." Thus the thought is of the separation wrought by death. Although, therefore, Peter does not explicitly speak of "dying to sin," it seems probable that this is his way of saying what Paul says in Romans 6. The contrast with *live* in the next clause confirms that this is the right understanding.

2:25 The translation strictly should be "For you were going astray like sheep," which brings out more strongly the fact that the readers had actually gone astray.

The pictures of conversion and healing are also joined together in the teaching based on Isaiah 6:10 in Matthew 13:15 and Mark 4:12.

secuted Christians should not retaliate), and it is included, as we argued above, in his positive understanding of the Christian's task in the world as the doing of good in society (2:14-15).

4. Retaliation meant as a deterrent too easily goes beyond "an eye for an eye." War all too easily gets out of control, and its value as deterrence may be totally lost in the lack of restraint and the spread of violence that it encourages. We may well ask whether it is possible for war (least of all, nuclear war) to be practiced with any sort of restraint. If not, it should be outlawed.

Wives and Husbands (3:1-7) In the second main part of the Household Code, Peter turns to the Christian duties of wives. Their problems receive much fuller attention than those of husbands, probably because Christian women were more likely to have non-Christian partners than Christian men and so were more liable to hostility. In fact Peter appears to assume that the men will have believing wives, and what he says here is intended to apply to all Christian wives and not just to those with unbelieving husbands.

The situation of the wife with the unbelieving husband is either one where the woman has been converted to Christianity after her marriage or where a Christian woman has had to enter upon an arranged marriage. In either case, it is extremely significant that a woman could have the freedom to adopt the Christian religion, regardless of whether she was under the will of her husband or parents.

The specific purpose of Peter's instructions to Christian wives with unbelieving husbands is to help them to bring them to faith. He assumes that the husband will not listen to, or has rejected, the preaching of the gospel. Three characteristics of the wife are commended: submission, beautiful character and freedom from fear.

Submission to Her Husband (3:1) Despite what has just been said, the custom of the time expected that a wife would be submissive to her husband, which means in part that she would normally adopt his religion. This placed converted wives in a difficult position. The Christian

Notes: 3:1 *In the same way* simply takes up the theme of submission that was already discussed in 2:13 and 18. This phrase does not put wives on the same level as slaves, but requires them to show submission in the way appropriate to their situation. Note that the wife should, therefore, seek to please her husband in other respects as much as possible. The basic command to submission sounds strange to modern Western readers, and so it must be understood in its first-century and early Christian context. Submission to the husband was the custom of the time. For Jews it was based on the stories of the Creation and Fall where the woman, originally created to be a helper for the man (Gen 2:20), is cursed by the pain of childbirth and submission to the rule of her husband (Gen 3:16).

In contrast, the Christian gospel emphasized that in the new situation brought about by the death and resurrection of Jesus "there is neither Jew nor Greek, slave nor free, male nor female, for you are all one in Christ Jesus" (Gal 3:28). Paul expresses the equality of husband and wife in as fundamental a matter as their physical sexual relationships (1 Cor 7:3-4). He also stresses that they are mutually dependent (1 Cor 11:11-12). This teaching clearly shows that the effects of the Fall are undone in the new creation that is manifested in the church.

Consequently, a new evaluation of the roles of husband and wife was bound to arise. With the new freedom that Christians enjoyed in Christ, there also inevitably arose the temptation to carry things to excess, trespassing the bounds of social propriety at that time. Christians had need for restraint so that they would not get the reputation for being libertines given to excess, such as happened with some extreme Protestant groups during the Reformation in their newfound freedom from the medieval church.

Peter reminds wives, therefore, to *submit* to their husbands; that is, to consider his needs and to fulfill them. (The husband, for his part, is reminded not to treat his wife as a chattel but to show her love and reverence, which will prevent him from making unreasonable and selfish demands on her.) Particularly in the mixed marriage the wife should be submissive to her husband so that the husband will not be put off from the gospel. As an unbeliever he is not yet ready to grant his wife the freedom given by a Christian husband. For the wife to claim that freedom unilaterally would be disastrous. She must exercise her freedom in Christ precisely by being willing to submit to the restraints imposed by her

same phrase is used in verse 7 to introduce the next section of the Household Code, addressed to husbands. (The teaching given here resembles that in Eph 5:22-24; Col 3:18; 1 Tim 2:9-15; and Tit 2:4-5.)

marriage to an unbeliever.

Although the equality of the sexes in Christ is the ideal, Christians still live in a fallen world and share in its fallenness. We are, as Martin Luther said, *"simul justi et peccatores"* (at the same time justified and sinful). Where the new law of love given by Christ is fulfilled, the relationships between husband and wife will partake of this quality. Each will treat the other with respect and reverence. But temptation to fall below the ideal is ever-present, and so wives and husbands need to be counseled accordingly.

Marital expectations today vary in different cultures and social groups. But everywhere the social institution of marriage carries with it certain obligations. We can argue that Peter is concerned with marital obligations that are recognized by society. Christians must uphold these, although they may go beyond them. For example, in a society which tolerates extramarital relationships on the part of husband or wife, the Christian will maintain a higher standard of marital fidelity. If a Christian woman is married to a Muslim man, she will have to restrain her freedom in Christ to accommodate herself to the obligations of Muslim marriage.

Some have suggested that Peter is really teaching wives to be subject not to their husbands but rather to the obligations of marriage in that culture. Alternatively, others propose that Peter is arguing that wives should observe the accepted social pattern for marriage of their time without the suggestion that submission to the husband is God's pattern for all time. Both of these interpretations are difficult to accept—the former because the texts speak of submission and obedience by the wives with no matching texts addressed to husbands, the latter because the command is given a basis in the will of God and its expression in Scripture.

It is a more promising approach to argue that the Christian husband will not make demands on his wife which reduce her to submission but that together they will seek God's will for their married life. In other words, the command here may be transcended in a Christian marriage, which makes the command unnecessary except perhaps as a fall-back

---

3:3 Warnings against feminine vanity and sexual provocation expressed in cosmetics and dress are well known in Scripture (Is 3:18-24; Prov 3:25-27; 1 Tim 2:9-10; Rev 17:4), and can also be paralleled from contemporary literature. See especially Balch (1981:101-102).

position. The command would then be analogous to those Old Testament laws that cease to be necessary when people follow the morality of the kingdom of God. For example, the law about keeping oaths that have been made to the Lord is no longer necessary when people let their yes be yes and their no be no without swearing an oath to confirm it. The law is there for people who cannot be trusted to tell the truth when not under oath, but it ceases to be effective when oaths are not required. We can also argue that submission in marriage was the type of moral conduct required of the wife at the time, certainly by Jews and also by many Gentiles. Christians were to live at least at that level.

Beauty of Character (3:2-6) Peter is concerned that Christian wives should commend themselves to their husbands and in society generally by the beauty of their character. Their lives will be characterized by purity and by reverence. The *reverence* is for the Lord (1:17; not for the husband, as in Eph 5:33) and indicates a desire to keep his commandments. This desire to obey should be their dominating motive and will result in a high moral standard. *Purity* refers to the maintenance of sexual morality.

Next, Peter argues that a wife's beauty does not come from the outward adornment of expensive hairstyles, jewelry and clothing. Notably Peter turns aside here from the de facto standards of the world (both then and now) where female adornment is socially acceptable, even fashionable. He follows a biblical precedent in condemning vanity and luxurious living. Had he lived today, he might well have commented on people who spend vast sums on clothes instead of giving to the poor, who do not even have food.

It is true that Peter's statement might well be translated: "Your beauty should *not so much* come from outward adornment . . . *but rather* it should be that of your inner self." Though desire to be beautiful and attractive is manifestly a commendable one, outward beauty, however much desirable, is secondary to beauty of character. The desire for outward beauty can easily lead to the sins of pride and vanity as well as of a wrong use of money. I wish that the indoctrination of young children

---

3:4 The thought that women should be gentle and quiet (1 Tim 2:2) is sometimes regarded as unacceptable in that it makes women out to be self-effacing and backward. One is tempted to wonder how the world would fare without the gentleness that is, on the whole, more successfully shown by women than by men.

on the importance of physical beauty in girls would cease. I have always felt sorry for the girl who has little outward beauty (as it is usually defined) and is made to feel inferior by foolish talk. What all women can have in Christ is beauty of character. Peter calls it a beauty of *the inner self,* but this translation is misleading. The inner self, of course, is not the invisible nature of the person but the whole person determined by the inner nature. Peter contrasts what a woman does with her outward appearance by her own effort and what is done by means of the divine gift that works outward from the inner personality. This is what matters to God, and his people should share his standards of judgment (compare 1 Sam 16:7; Mt 6:4, 6, 18). Peter commends a gentle and quiet spirit, a characteristic found in Jesus himself (Mt 11:29; 21:5). It is *imperishable* in that it cannot fade away, like physical beauty or outward adornment, but is lasting and therefore all the more valuable.

Peter backs up what he is saying by appealing to the example of the saintly women in the Old Testament (vv. 5-6). Since they put their trust in God, they were freed from the need to depend on human resources of beauty. Instead they made themselves beautiful in that they showed a gentle and quiet spirit. This expressed itself in submission to their husbands, a conspicuous example of which was Sarah, the wife of Abraham, who addressed him as *master.* The Greek word used here corresponds to the Hebrew word *'adon,* which was used for lords and masters of all kinds. (The Hebrew word which is normally used for "husband" is *ba'al,* which has the force of "master, owner.")

I once asked a class of students, which included married men, whether they and their wives took this example literally and seriously. One of them said that at the beginning of their married life his wife had indeed done so. "What happened?" I asked. He answered, "It didn't last for very long!" And yet Peter encourages Christian wives to show that they are

---

3:5 *Hope* is not very far removed from faith and trust in God. It is typical of Peter's theological vocabulary. See 1:3.

3:6 For the thought of being the offspring of Abraham see Matthew 3:9; Romans 4:11-12; James 2:21.

3:7 For similar teaching addressed to husbands see 1 Thessalonians 4:4-5.

The weaker partner is literally "the weaker vessel." Some commentators interpret this to mean the woman as a sexual object, drawing attention to 1 Thessalonians 4:4, where the

the spiritual daughters of Sarah by following her example, especially by doing what is good (NIV *what is right*). Mutual respect is surely the modern counterpart (5:5).

Freedom from Fear (3:6) The third thing wives are commanded to do is not to be afraid of anything that might terrify them. They are to fear God (3:2), not their husbands. Their obedience to their husbands should not arise from fear. If they trust in God, they will not be afraid of anything that a pagan husband—or, for that matter, a Christian one who does not act in a Christian manner—may do to them. The fear of God is a positive attitude which is accompanied by hope in him (3:5).

Husbands (3:7) After all this, the husbands are addressed *in the same way.* The force of the phrase is that they are to fulfill their particular role in the social relationship of marriage, just as the wives are to fulfill theirs. Marriage imposes obligations on both partners. They are to show consideration as they live with their wives. The reference is to the whole of their life together, and it may well specifically include their physical relationships (compare 1 Cor 7:1-5). It is a temptation to men to impose their physical desires on their wives regardless of the latter's ability to cope.

Christian men should show some insight, a human virtue that is also demanded by the character of Christian love which includes respect for the loved person as a person. Both husband and wife are physically weak beings who can become tired and weary. In general, although she will probably live longer than her husband, the wife is physically the weaker of the two. She is particularly so before and after childbirth, therefore she must be treated with respect.

Though she is weaker physically, she is just as much as her husband the object of God's grace. They share together in the hope of eternal life to come and in the present experience of that grace. Such a sharing together in the Christian life will express itself in praying together—and

---

same Greek word *(skeuos)* can also refer to the wife as a sexual object (as with similar rabbinic usage). But this interpretation is almost certainly wrong in 1 Thessalonians 4:4. Here the fact that Peter says the wife is the *weaker* vessel shows that he has in mind her comparative physical weakness compared with the man. The thought too widens out from that of physical sexual relationships and emphasizes the need for gentleness on the part of the husband in all aspects of the marriage relationship.

To narrow down *your prayers* to those of the husbands only (Grudem 1988:145) is unjustified.

there is no suggestion that the wife had to pray silently or wear a head-covering! If there is a lack of love and the husband is forcing his will on his wife, or she is responding in kind, how can they possibly pray together in harmony?

There is a danger in the feminist mood of today that some people will jettison such a passage as this from their working canon of Scripture. Some may do so blatantly, but evangelical Christians are more likely to ignore it quietly. The instructions remain authoritative for us today, but they need to be translated into terms suitable for the modern situation. It is in no way inconsistent with acceptance of the full authority of Scripture to seek to determine just what it is saying to us today.

Even in today's world, where the bond is interpreted in a rather loose fashion, marriage still imposes obligations on both partners. There is a higher ideal for the Christian: Christian marriage must be based on a mutual love that treats the partner with respect and honor. Peter here establishes Christian marriage on the highest possible level as the loving union of two persons who share together and equally in the promises of God. He assumes that husband and wife will pray together. They do not live separate Christian lives, but they share together in the deepest relationship of their life.

Even where only one of the partners is a Christian, the relationship should still be marked by love and respect. The love of the Christian partner will include something of the love of God himself for those who have not yet responded to his grace. The Christian partner who feels this love for an unconverted spouse is obligated to live in such a way as to commend the Christian faith to him or her.

And although we live in a world in which women occupy roles of leadership in society and in the church that were largely unknown in the first century, it is surely still the case that a quiet spirit is preferable to a raucous, unmannerly character. If the effeminate man acts unnaturally for his sex, so too does the woman who tries to be masculine.

Finally, we may well be tempted by the world around us to seek self-expression in vanity and expensive living when modesty and charity are the desired Christian virtues to be cultivated. And, although Peter's remarks on the temptations to pride and luxury are addressed especially to women, they are just as applicable to men today.

General Instructions (3:8-12) The third part of the Household Code contains instructions addressed to all the members of the church. They are quite brief and are backed by a quotation from Psalm 34:13-17, the same psalm that was already quoted in 2:3.

In verse 8 Peter is clearly thinking of relationships between fellow Christians. It is interesting how, having begun with the duties of Christians to other members of their household, whether Christian or non-Christian, Peter now finishes with teaching for the "household of faith." In verse 9, however, he implicitly reverts to the relation of the Christian to other people in general, as he considers how Christians should respond to hostility. Clearly Peter does not draw hard and fast distinctions between attitudes toward Christians and non-Christians. There is no double standard.

Once again, Peter's teaching is not peculiar to himself. Behind what he says lie the words of Jesus in Luke 6:27-28: "But I tell you who hear me: Love your enemies, do good to those who hate you, bless those who curse you, pray for those who mistreat you." There is similar teaching in Romans 12:10, 14-17; 1 Thessalonians 5:13-15 (compare Col 3:12-15; Eph 4:1-3, 31-32).

The Mutual Qualities of Christians (3:8) What is required of Christians in their mutual relationships?

1. They should *live in harmony with one another.* The Greek word (literally, "to be of like mind") means that Christians should have the same basic aim of serving God and loving one another, instead of being guided by individual, selfish interests. This is important advice in a world where individualism holds sway and everybody is encouraged to do his own thing. Obviously Peter does not mean that each person has identical aims, but rather that the dominant aim of every Christian must be the same, namely to love and serve God, and that other aims are derived from and subordinate to this one.

Christians, therefore, will work together and not act in isolation. Rather than competing with each other's interests they will help one another to achieve what is God's will for their lives. In other words, if I believe that God is calling me to do something particular in my life, then it must harmonize with my duties toward other Christians in helping them to do what God calls them to do. I must resist the temptation to think that my specific calling from God is so important that I must not allow concern for other people's needs to deter me from pursuing it.

2. Christians should *be sympathetic.* The etymology of the word suggests that it means "suffering with" other people, that is, entering into their experiences to share the joy or lessen the sorrow. Paul puts the point more vividly and concretely when he says, "Rejoice with those who rejoice; mourn with those who mourn" (Rom 12:15; compare Ecclus 7:34). The secret of sympathizing surely lies in relating so closely to others that we feel what happens to them as something that is happening to us. And that means willingness to surrender our independence. To be sure, there are limits set. What Peter means here is having the strength of character to set personal feelings on one side and enter into the experience of others, rather than becoming dependent on other people (though clearly we are strengthened by the corresponding sympathy of other people for us). Again, there is the danger of becoming a busybody, interfering in other people's lives.

3. Christians should also *love as brothers,* a quality already commended in 1:22. Again we have a component of common Christian instruction (Rom 12:10; 1 Thess 4:9; Heb 13:1; 2 Pet 1:7). Though basic to all that is commended in this section, here it takes its place as one aspect of the total picture. The ideal Christian community is one which produces between people who have no blood ties the same bonds of affection as are expected between brothers (Ps 133:1).

4. Christians should *be compassionate,* showing loving consideration to people who are in need instead of ignoring them (Eph 4:32). Here the word suggests that they should have actual feelings of concern for others which are then expressed in action. It is sometimes said that love as an emotion cannot be commanded, and indeed often we can do little more than give or act for the sake of the destitute without having any personal concern or involvement with individuals (how could we, when there are so many of them and it is beyond human ability to relate

---

Notes: **3:8** There is some disagreement whether Peter is still giving advice for life within the family (Balch 1981:86-90) or more broadly within the church. If Peter was thinking of house-church groups, the boundary would be a very fluid one.

In harmony (Gk *homophrōn*) is found only here, but the same thought is expressed in other words in Romans 12:16 (the whole of vv. 8-9 have parallels in Rom 12:9-18); Romans 15:5; Philippians 2:2 and 4:2 (where the phrase "to think the same thing/the one thing

personally to each one?). But if it is possible—as it unfortunately is—for people deliberately to harden their hearts against the needs of others, surely it is also possible for the Christian to learn to become more compassionate and loving to the needy. Here the focus in any case is on caring for those in the Christian community, and the point may well be that we need to learn to love those who are in poorer circumstances than ourselves despite the very natural temptation to love the people who occupy a similar station in life to ourselves.

5. If we are to fulfill these injunctions, we will also have to be *humble*. Humble people are those who are conscious of their own position as God's creatures, entirely dependent on him, and therefore who are able to think more highly of others than of themselves. But again this needs some elucidation. Suppose that there is no doubt that Mary is better than John at mathematics (as measured by objective tests) or in morality (as measured by court convictions). It would be false and indeed wrong for Mary to say that she thought more highly of John as a mathematician than of herself. Assessments of people's relative ability and character for appointments to positions are necessary (who will be the better accountant or the more honest security guard?). Is it, then, merely comparisons involving oneself that are excluded? Certainly not.

Surely Peter's point is that we must not make differences between people as persons; we must not regard ourselves as better persons than others. But does that restrict the scope of the command to a narrow area? Does it apply merely to agreeing that the other person should get into the lifeboat before me unless I possess better navigational skills that will ensure the safety of the other survivors in the boat? The casuist can easily dream up cases of this kind. Further, we have the impossible situation of two Christians, each of whom puts the other first, and stalemate results. It is impossible for any one of two utterly deferential people to persuade the other to go through a doorway first!

Perhaps the solution is to fall back on Paul's clearer and fuller injunc-

---

among one another" is found).

Humble (Gk *tapeinophrōn*) is an adjective peculiar to Peter in the New Testament. In the secular world it had the bad sense of "faint-hearted" or "feeble-minded," but in the Greek Old Testament it is used once in a good sense (Prov 29:23) to contrast the humble man with the proud person. The simple adjective *tapeinos* has much the same meaning (see 5:5). For the corresponding noun see 5:5.

tion: "Do not think of yourself more highly than you ought, but rather think of yourself with sober judgment" (Rom 12:3). Appropriate considerations must be taken into account: I may be a better mathematician than Y, but that does not entitle me to a better standing in life than her. I must love her equally as God's creation, equally as the object of God's love (he has no favorites) and equally as the object of my love.

Relationships with Non-Christians (3:9) With verse 9 we move on to behavior that is more clearly related to non-Christians than to fellow Christians. When similar teaching is given elsewhere, it always refers to the relations of Jesus' followers to those who attack them. The same must be true here, even though it is possible that similar situations could arise between believers. The basic rule is that if people treat you badly, you should not pay them back in the same coin.

The principle attacked here is one that is engraved in fallen human nature: vengeance. In situations where the detailed maintenance of law and order by the community did not exist, private revenge was the normal expectation. Ancient lawgivers had to insist that it must not be greater than the original provocation—for example, an eye for an eye.

The humane substitution of a monetary penalty for a bodily injury did not affect the basic principle. Advances were made in two ways. First, private revenge was replaced by community justice, in which the community, acting (however imperfectly) as the agent of God, administered a legally defined penalty. Second, the teaching of Jesus forebade the claiming of personal revenge for all those wrongs that fell outside the sphere of the law. Christians recognized that especially where they were being wronged for the sake of Christ, it was all the more essential that they should refrain from retaliation. And this applied in the case of evil deeds as well as of insulting language. Jesus was their example (2:23). On the contrary, they were to seize the opportunity for witness by giving a blessing instead of abuse (Lk 6:28; Rom 12:14, 17; 1 Cor 4:12; 1 Thess 5:15). If Jewish wisdom already recognized the folly of paying back evil for good (Prov 17:13), Jesus emphasized the need to repay good for evil.

3:10-12 This quotation is an interesting example of how Christians, having found relevant teaching for themselves in one part of the Old Testament, would go back to it (see 2:3 above) and comb it more thoroughly for further helpful teaching.

But what is *blessing?* Surely it is not just saying soothing things or mouthing vaguely, "May the Lord bless you." It must rather be a case of offering the gospel with its promises of divine blessings to persecutors so that they have the chance to respond to it and actually receive the blessings. But Peter has more than only the persecutors in mind. We could easily narrow down the list of possible recipients of blessing if we confined it to deliberate persecutors, but all kinds of people hand out evil and abuse and not just to Christians.

Peter inserts a reason for such conduct: *To this you were called, so that you may inherit a blessing.* Christians are called by God to this non-retaliatory way of life, which offers blessings to other people, as the condition or way by which they themselves will receive blessing from God. Put otherwise, you yourself will not receive a blessing from God unless you are willing to share his blessing with other people. Stated thus, the reason for blessing other people could be regarded as a selfish one: I do good to others to get God's blessing in my own life. But the motive is surely not meant to be construed in this way. The point is rather that Peter tells the Christian that inherent in the Christian way of life is the attitude of love for others, including enemies and persecutors. If you are not willing to share God's gifts, you show that you are not worthy to receive them yourself.

Scriptural Backing (3:10-12) This last appeal is strengthened and confirmed by a quotation—the longest in the epistle—from Psalm 34, although it is not formally introduced as a citation. Peter's logic is: if you want to have God's blessing, do not speak evil or do evil, but do what is good. The Lord shows favor to the righteous but is opposed to those who do evil. Thus the quotation justifies the way of life in verse 9 by pointing out that it leads to divine blessing. It appeals to the universal longing for personal benefits and shows how they may be obtained. This type of apparent merit-teaching is not uncommon in the Bible. Essentially it commends righteousness as a way of life and warns against unrighteousness. Our behavior matters.

Nothing that the Bible says elsewhere about undeserved grace can

---

The Greek phrase translated *Whoever would love life and see good days* is slightly odd (literally, "he who wishes to love life and to see good days"). The Hebrew of the psalm is literally "which man takes delight in life [and] loves days to see good?" The Septuagint,

alter this fact. The whole point of undeserved grace and salvation by faith alone is that it comes in a context of broken laws and unfulfilled righteousness, ethical ideals that have not been attained. Nothing suggests that these ideals no longer matter, that divine grace and forgiveness have rendered righteousness unnecessary or irrelevant. The point of grace is that it forgives transgressions of the law; it does not state that the law does not matter.

The quotation is apt for Peter's purpose, and the whole of it is germane to it. The basis for the appeal lies in the last verse quoted which affirms that the eyes of the Lord are on the righteous. References to God's eyes often indicate simply that he is all-seeing (Heb 4:13) and judges everybody (Prov 15:3; compare Ps 11:4; 2 Sam 11:13). But they can also indicate, as here, that he views the righteous and those who fear him with favor (Ps 33:18-19; 34:15; compare Deut 11:12; contrast Is 1:15). The pairing of the ears with the eyes is not uncommon and simply reinforces the thought.

Hebrew poetic parallelism has often been thought to offer simply direct synonyms or antonyms, but it is now recognized that the second clause can add something fresh to the first one. We may perhaps detect the thought that God actively listens for the cries of his people in their need. The word for "prayer" here is specifically the word for "petition." The "righteous" in the language of the Psalms are those who stand in a right covenant relationship to God and trust in him. Such a relationship is expressed in appropriate behavior. Conversely, God's face is against those who do evil. Again we have an anthropomorphic metaphor. God is said to turn his face toward his people and let it shine upon them. He turns his face away from the wicked, but at other times, as here, he is said to turn his face against them (Lev 17:10; Ezek 14:8). There is no inconsistency, but merely the use of different existing human metaphors which express disregard and positive wrath respectively.

God's attitude thus depends on the attitudes and corresponding actions demonstrated by people toward him. The positive outcome of

---

following a slightly different Hebrew text for the last phrase, has "who is the man who wishes life, loving to see good days?" Peter has simplified the expression. He has abandoned the question form in the psalm. He has also altered the construction from *thelōn zōēn, agapōn idein* to *thelōn zōēn agapan kai idein*. Possibly he has used the verb *agapaō* in the sense "to enjoy," corresponding to the Hebrew *haphets* (compare Ecclus 4:12), perhaps

God's attitude to the righteous is that they live a life which can be enjoyed and experience good.

The specific nature of righteous conduct is now spelled out. There is appropriately a reference to the need for right use of the tongue in general. The righteous person must refrain from whatever is evil—a wide expression that is filled out in the detailed speech ethics in the letter of James (especially 1:26; 3:1-12)—and especially from deceit. The thought of deceit is not germane to Peter's immediate topic, but fits in with an earlier line of thought in 2:1 (compare 2:22). Then the thought widens out to conduct in general in terms of turning away from evil and doing good. More specifically, the psalmist encourages his readers to seek peace and pursue it. *Pursue* expresses vigorous effort to attain something (Prov 15:9; Hos 6:3).

☐ **The Christian Attitude toward Hostility (3:13—5:11)**
Reading a letter intended for somebody else inevitably means that what it has to say may not be directly relevant to us. Words of love written to another probably say little about the author's attitude toward me. Instructions written for people in a different situation from us may be irrelevant to us. Peter was writing to people who were facing sharp hostility from their employers, their neighbors, people at large, and possibly also government officials. We may not face this persecution, but Christians around the world are in just that kind of situation. Peter's words are directiy relevant when allowance is made for differences in comparatively minor points (for instance, that slavery of the ancient kind no longer exists).

Again, Christians in Aberdeen or Abilene or Amsterdam, because they are less likely to share these ancient readers' situation, may feel that Peter is on a different wavelength. They may even try to exaggerate or twist their perception of their own situation in the hope that this will make the letter more meaningful to them. But for those of us who live where religious toleration generally rules, Peter's teaching is still highly rele-

---

because he did not like the use of *thelō* with a noun as object.

The phrase *seek peace and pursue it* seems to be unparalleled outside the psalm. It is probably just a strong way of encouraging people to promote peace and to refrain from strife. The same language, probably ultimately drawn from the psalm, is found in Romans 14:19 and Hebrews 12:14.

vant. What he says to Christians who are actively and vigorously attacked for their faith applies to us whose Christianity is ignored and quietly tolerated. Maintaining the highest standards of Christian living and seizing every opportunity for positive witness are abiding obligations of Christians.

A last major section of the letter begins here. From this point onward Peter is concerned principally (but not exclusively) with the Christians' response to actual persecution. To be sure, the hostile attitude of non-Christian society was also very much in the background in earlier parts of the letter (see 1:6; 2:12, 15, 19; 3:1, 9), but there he focused directly on the character of Christians individually, in the Christian community and in various social relationships. Now the focus shifts to an actual response to specific attacks.

The section extends to 5:11 and can be broken down into seven subsections. In 3:13-17, Peter urges his readers to make positive use of the opportunities posed by hostile situations. Then, just as he had reinforced his teaching to slaves facing the possibility of suffering (2:18-20) by reference to what Jesus suffered (vv. 21-25), here he reinforces his teaching by reference to the suffering and the victory of Jesus (3:18-22). This is followed by encouragement to the readers not to lapse back into pagan ways (4:1-6) and then by an appeal for mutual love and concern evidenced by serving one another in the congregation (4:7-11). There is a pause in the exhortation here, punctuated by a brief doxology, and then Peter returns to the topic. Again he describes suffering as a form of testing and urges Christians to face it in the right spirit (4:12-19). Then he comments once more on the topic of church life, mentioning especially the need for good leadership (5:1-5). Finally he urges the readers to resist the devil, who is active in attacking them, and to commit themselves into the safekeeping of God (5:6-11).

The Blessings and Opportunities of the Persecuted (3:13- 17) A

cartoon strip that appeared in our church bulletin showed a man reciting

---

Notes: 3:13 Verse 13 is linked to verse 9 rather than to verses 10-12.

Eager in Greek is *zēlōtēs,* a word used for enthusiasts, especially for Jews who were enthusiastic partisans for God's law and the temple (Acts 21:20; 22:3; Gal 1:14). Here the point is that Christians do good not simply because it is their duty but because they want to do it.

various biblical passages which assure us that the Lord will take care of us and protect us from fear. In the last frame the dentist's receptionist says to him, "Dr. Jones is ready for you now, sir," at which he breaks into a cold sweat. Fear of physical pain is strong in most of us, and quoting biblical texts like "The Lord is my helper, whom shall I fear?" does not always drive it away.

Equally strong is the fear of hostile attitudes, of being cold-shouldered and ignored, of suffering loss of face and much else. Peter did not need to tell his readers that they might suffer for being Christians; they had already experienced it. When he said to them, *Do not repay evil with evil, or insult with insult* (3:9), he referred to situations that had already arisen. A taste of opposition was enough to make them fear for the future. Against that background, Christians could well worry about what perse-cution they would endure for being Christians and ask what good it would do them in the long run. Some must have shrunk from certain actions for fear of the consequences, persuading themselves that these lines of action weren't really worth following anyhow. Because of this fear Peter begins this section by taking up the question: What will happen to us if we live as Christians?

Be Eager to Do Good (3:13) On the whole, Christians are not so likely to suffer. The people who suffer most are those who do wrong and suffer the penalties inflicted on evildoers. It is the slave who displeases his master by failing to do his work properly or by stealing his property who will get into trouble. But the Christian, simply because he is a Christian, lives a different kind of life. He is *eager to do good.* "Doing good" means following the Christian way of life as it has been developed earlier in the letter (see especially 3:11).

This lifestyle would conform in many ways with the standards of pagan morality. Christians should not mistakenly assume that only they have standards of goodness or try to live up to them—that the rest of the world lives in the darkness of unrelieved immorality. In fact what Peter says here could well apply to the world in which many of us live, where

---

Another interpretation of this verse reads: "If you do good, nobody can *really* harm you" (compare 2 Tim 4:18). That is to say, you will suffer bodily harm, but it cannot really hurt you because they cannot touch your spirit. This interpretation, though true as a principle, is inappropriate here, since it gives a bad connection with verse 14.

Christian morality may not seem to be too different from non-Christian morality, and where, as a result, Christians do not stand out. Truly there will be important differences. As Peter goes on to say, our way of life is *good behavior in Christ* (3:16), which means that our submission to his rule and imitation of his example should engender a life of a different quality from pagans. Nevertheless, insofar as Christian morality is in harmony with worldly morality, the world will recognize and approve it. It will note that Christians are *eager* to practice it. So much so that Peter can ask rhetorically, "If you do good, will anybody try to cause you bodily harm?" In general, those who do the right thing will not be attacked.

The Possibility of Suffering (3:14) Verse 13 stated what is only a general rule, and general rules can have exceptions. Doing good may lead, in certain circumstances, to hostile attacks. The Christian standard of righteousness may not be acceptable to the surrounding world. As I write, some Christians are suffering verbal abuse for suggesting that the simplest (and cheapest) prophylactic against the spread of AIDS is the practice of Christian sexual morality—which holds that the only context for the right enjoyment of sexual intercourse is heterosexual marriage. Today some opponents of Christianity reject any kind of moral standards and react violently against those who uphold them. What happens then?

Christians should claim the promise of Jesus whose wording is echoed here: "Blessed are those who are persecuted because of righteousness" (Mt 5:10). Those who suffer for being Christians receive gracious gifts from God, which more than compensate for the suffering. God's Spirit rests upon them (1 Pet 4:14). The thought, therefore, is definitely not confined to bliss in the next world but includes spiritual blessings that God's people receive from him in this life. This prospect puts the sufferings caused by persecution into perspective.

Freedom from Fear (3:14-15) Fortified by the promise above,

3:14 Peter uses the somewhat unusual optative mood of the Greek verb here and in 3:17 to express a rare contingency; later in 4:14 he is much more definite about the possibility.

The phraseology in verses 14-15 is based on Isaiah 8:12-13: "Do not fear what they fear, and do not dread it. The Lord Almighty is the one you are to regard as holy, he is the one you are to fear, he is the one you are to dread." The Greek is literally "do not fear the fear of them." The NIV text has "do not fear what they fear" in conformity with Isaiah 8:12. A marginal note suggests, "do not fear their threats" (threats as the fear-inspiring object that they put before you). But the Greek could simply mean "Do not be afraid of them." Note how Peter, having quoted from Isaiah 8 in 2:8, now returns to that chapter.

Christians must take positive attitudes toward the threats that they face. They need not be afraid or alarmed. The patient awaiting treatment from the dentist may well get the courage and endurance to face physical discomfort from the knowledge that it is the price for long-term relief from the agony of chronic toothache. Sportsplayers will put up with injuries on the field that they wouldn't if inflicted for no good reason off the field. The more conscious Christians are of the blessings promised by God to his people the more they will see suffering in a different way.

In fact, instead of being afraid of people, Christians' minds should be dominated by their heavenly Lord. Jesus told his disciples not to fear what their enemies might do to them, but rather to fear God, who has the power to destroy people in Gehenna (Mt 10:28 = Lk 12:4-5). Peter is encouraging people who need no such stern warnings, and so he continues in verse 15 in a positive vein, still drawing on Isaiah 8. To hallow Christ as Lord means to have an inward attitude of obedience to him that dictates our behavior in the world. Christians will not act in any way that will bring dishonor on Christ or suggest that they do not reverence him as Lord.

Readiness to Bear Witness (3:15-16) With this inner motive of obedience to Christ, the Christian should seize the opportunities of witness presented in situations of persecution. There will be occasions when Christians are directly asked about their Christian commitment. The picture is not necessarily one of appearances in court (though it may be included) but of less formal questioning, which can be more difficult to cope with. It may be easier to speak for Christ in the dock than on the spot among sophisticated, worldly people.

The object of investigation is the Christian's hope, which, as Peter's synonym for faith, stresses the element of future expectation (1:3, 21).

3:15 Christians must *set apart* or "hallow" Christ as Lord. The phrase is similar to the petition in the Lord's Prayer, "Hallowed be thy Name," which is addressed to God. The text in Isaiah 8:13 speaks of regarding the Lord Almighty as holy. By adding the words "the Christ" Peter applies to Jesus what was originally said with respect to God, a clear indication of how Jesus was ranked alongside God the Father by the early Christians (and yet not identified with him; see 1:3).

The phrase *asks you to give a reason* was a current Greek idiom for "requiring a legal defense," but the usage here is broader.

This may have been particularly noteworthy to outsiders. And their interest should gladly be grasped as an opportunity for a positive, reasoned presentation of the gospel.

The text probably implies no more than that Christians should always seize such opportunities when they arise, but it is fair to add that they will be unable to capitalize on the opportunities if they are not already prepared with a coherent understanding of faith and some practice in rehearsing it. Jesus' saying in Matthew 10:19 is meant to rule out worry, not preparation!

In impromptu "interrogations" the temptation to reply sharply would be strong. As we have already seen, such illustrations can readily be found in the accounts of the trials and deaths of Jewish martyrs. Christians, however, must respond *with gentleness and respect* (literally, "fear"). Gentleness should be shown toward the antagonists and respect emphatically toward God (otherwise we would have a sharp contradiction with 3:14). The former quality surely implies that the aim of answering is evangelistic—the conversion of the opponents. Paul is a good example of this attitude in Acts 26:25-32, as King Agrippa fully recognized (v. 28). In the context of this letter, a gentle response is in harmony with Christians' general pattern of behavior, maintaining a conscience that does not condemn them (compare 3:21). Of course, this does not necessarily mean that they have lived a perfect life in every detail.

It is this gentle behavior that excites opprobrium from non-Christians. But now they are puzzled by the way in which the Christians respond to their slander, and the hoped-for result is that they will be ashamed of their earlier attitudes. Peter says that the demeanor of Christians on trial for their faith should make those who formerly jeered at them think again as they are confronted by their gracious attitudes. Possibly he is thinking of the way in which persecutors will be ashamed at the Last Judgment when they realize that the people whom they despised are honored by God. More likely he has in mind a change of heart by the persecutors here in this life.

The Better Way (3:17) Finally, Peter again makes the point that it is better to suffer for doing good than for doing evil. The statement is a proverbial one and could simply mean that it is morally better to suffer at the hands of ignorant and evil people for doing good than to bear one's punishment for having done evil. But Peter writes in a Christian context. Surely he means that, if we are going to suffer at all, it is better to suffer persecution than to be punished for breaking the law (2:19-20; 4:15-16). Such patient endurance of persecution is a powerful form of Christian witness. It is also possible that Peter means that to suffer persecution from men for doing good is better than to incur God's judgment for doing wrong (Michaels 1988:191-92).

The Significance of Christ's Victory (3:18-22)

A glance at the religion section in any secular bookstore will reveal that people today are interested in astrology, magic and the occult rather than in Christianity. Fascination with the supernatural, coupled with a natural fear of it, prevails despite the scientific materialism of our age.

The early Christians also lived in a society that really believed in the existence of spiritual powers, both good and evil. Obviously the New Testament writers shared this belief. It was entirely natural, therefore, for Peter to perceive the persecution of Christians as motivated not merely by the malice of pagan masters, neighbors and rulers but by sinister demonic forces behind them. Was it not when Satan entered into him that Judas made preparations to betray Jesus (Lk 22:3; Jn 13:2)? And when natural disasters hit them as well, they were all the more likely to believe that behind all their sufferings lay the influence of opposing demonic powers.

Demon-initiated persecution raised the question of the power of God to give his people the upper hand. One type of answer to the whole problem might well have been to deny the existence of such beings. That way was not open to the New Testament writers; the existence of Satan and other evil powers was taken for granted by both Jesus and his followers.

There are, to be sure, people today who would nevertheless hold to this position and argue that the existence of evil nonmaterial powers is mere superstition. Science, they would say, rules out the existence of such beings. This claim is of course partly true: there are a lot of superstitions around which are the product of sheer imagination and which can be shown to be false. But to agree with materialists thus far is not necessarily to deny that there is "something" (or "somebody") at work in the world which lies outside the sphere of scientific investigation.

A more acceptable modern type of approach might therefore be to say that the biblical "powers" represent an attempt to conceptualize the forces opposed to God and goodness. They depict the forces of evil in the language of an existing mythology which we can reinterpret today. But to say this or something like it is emphatically not to deny the existence of an evil power that is superhuman or transcendent and tremendously powerful; it is only to say that we can also express it in other terms. And it is significant that some modern theologians, who would deny any crudely literal understanding of the demonic, nevertheless would insist that the language points to a reality that threatens human existence.

If, then, we accept that "angels, authorities and powers" stand for something real, what is the power of that reality? This is the question that Peter raises and answers in this part of his letter, a paragraph whose original meaning is as difficult to discover as that of any passage in the New Testament and which appears to speak a language far removed from modern people.

Although it is the problem of the nature of the evil powers which strikes the attention of the reader, we must remember that Peter's main purpose in this section is to encourage his readers to face persecution fearlessly and positively by showing them the significance of Jesus. He points out that their situation is like that of Jesus who also had to suffer for having done good. But, although it may seem that he is presenting Jesus as an example to follow, in fact much more than his example is being presented here. He links the resurrection and ascension of Jesus

---

Notes: 3:18 The connection with the preceding paragraph is debated: (1) Christ is presented as an example of suffering for doing good (3:17), to confirm that if even he had to suffer in this way, his followers can expect the same; (2) he may be an example of courageous preaching to be followed by Christians who are to bear witness (3:15-16) when they are persecuted (if he preached to the evil spirits, Christians should witness to their persecutors); (3) above all, the death of Jesus and his triumphant resurrection give a theological basis to the suffering of Christians and assure them of ultimate victory over the forces of evil manifested in persecution.

There is a similarity between this passage and 2:21-25 where Peter moves from the thought of Christ as example to Christ as Savior. Many commentators have argued that Peter is quoting an existing Christian hymn at this point and has added fresh phrases to it to suit

with his victory over the powers of evil, and in doing so refers to the victorious proclamation of Jesus to the disobedient spirits associated with the time of the flood. They are particularly singled out for mention because despite their activity at that time God saved Noah and his family *through water*, and a correspondence can be seen between that situation and the way in which baptism now saves Christian believers.

The Suffering of Jesus (3:18) Peter uses language which shows that he is thinking of the death of Jesus in terms of atonement for sin.

1. The verb *died*, following directly after Peter's use of *suffered* in verse 17, expresses the painful, undeserved death of Jesus on the cross (Lk 17:25; Acts 1:3; Heb 13:12).

2. Peter states that his death took place *once*. This could mean "at one point in time" and hence finite in duration; but it is more probable that the phrase, correctly rendered by NIV as "once for all," denotes its uniqueness as the one act that secures forgiveness (Rom 6:10; compare Heb 7:27; 9:12, 26, 28; 10:10). It does not need repetition, unlike the annual Jewish sacrifices.

3. Jesus died *for sins*. This phrase is found in Galatians 1:4 (with equivalents in 1 Cor 15:3 and Heb 10:12) and is derived from language used in the Greek Old Testament, where it refers to the effects of sacrifices. The death of Jesus is like a sacrifice in that it takes away sin and cancels its effects. Sin no longer stands between sinners and God to render them liable to judgment. The reference to the fact that he was himself righteous, which is the human equivalent to an unblemished sacrifice (1:19), shows that the idea of sacrifice is present here.

Indeed, we may well ask what other idea is likely to have been present in an author whose thought is so clearly molded by the Old Testament

---

his present purpose. Not all agree, however, on how to reconstruct a hypothetical original source. The most that we can say is that Peter is probably using existing traditions. In any case, it is likely that every word counts with Peter, especially since he does exactly the same thing in 2:21-22, and that he is here deliberately stating a doctrine of atonement and victory. Peter is the kind of person who rejoices in the thought of the cross and what it achieved.

In place of *died*, some textual evidence warrants the variant *suffered*, which is Peter's usual verb (2:19, 21, 23; 4:1). It also links the thought more clearly to the suffering of Christians. Scribes could easily have assimilated the text to Peter's usual phraseology or, alternatively, they could have altered the verb to the one which was more customary in theological statements about the saving action of Jesus. (The same textual problem arises in 2:21, but there the textual evidence is much stronger for *suffered*.)

and whose sacrificial understanding of the death of Jesus has already been made clear (1:19; 2:24).

4. The positive result of Jesus' death is to bring sinners, now set free from sin, to God (Rom 5:1-2; Eph 2:18; 3:12; Heb 10:19-22). Those who were formerly prevented from entering the holy presence of God because of their unrighteousness may now do so. They can bring their prayers and praises to him. Doubtless Peter thinks of spiritual access to God, but he may also look forward to the ultimate destiny of the Christian.

5. Finally, Peter emphasizes that Christ acted as the righteous one on behalf of unrighteous people. This phrase brings out the parallel between Christians, who suffer simply because they are disliked by the world, and Jesus, who also suffered innocently. Clearly the phrase says more than it needs to make this point, because it alludes to the vicarious character of Christ's death. He died on behalf of the unrighteous so that they might obtain salvation.

But Peter is not concerned simply to spell out a doctrine of atonement for its own sake. Why should he want to do that in the present context of helping persecuted Christians? He wants, rather, to emphasize the status of believers, who now have access to God and can call on him in their need with confidence.

The Death and Resurrection of Jesus (3:18) The sentence in verse 18 continues without a break in the Greek, and Peter adds a pair of deliberately contrasting phrases. They tell us that Christ was put to death and brought to life. Taking the verbs without considering the qualifying phrases *in the body* and *by the Spirit,* we cannot avoid the conclusion that they refer to the death of Jesus and to his resurrection

---

The interpretation of "flesh" and "spirit" in the NIV text is not the most usual or the most likely one. The form of the Greek sentence strongly suggests that both phrases should be construed in the same syntactical manner ("in flesh . . . in spirit") instead of in different ways ("in the body . . . by the Spirit").

There are basically two other possibilities:

1. The parallel phrasing has often been thought to denote the two constituents of the being of Jesus, either his body and his soul, or his human nature and his divine nature. Both ideas should be rejected.

The former would suggest that only the body of Jesus died and only his soul was brought to life, which is contrary to the New Testament belief in the resurrection of the body. This view would be tenable only if the phrases referred not to the resurrection of Jesus but to

respectively. The first verb refers not to dying naturally but to being put to death. It is used in Mark 14:55 of the crucifixion of Jesus.

The second verb similarly cannot refer to somebody reviving or coming to life again through their own power but is passive and refers to being brought back to life by an outside agency. This can only designate God's bringing of Jesus back to life. This fits with the witness of the New Testament: no writer ever says that Jesus raised himself from the dead but that God raised him. (When Jn 10:18 attributes to Jesus the authority to take up his life again, this is only because he has been commanded to do so by God. The point is that the ultimate authority over the death and life of Jesus does not lie with men.)

By adding these two verbs in verse 18 Peter emphasizes that the saving action of Christ, through which he brings people to God, lies not only in his death but also in his resurrection (compare 1:3; 3:22). These two historical acts belong together as parts of one single saving action.

What are we to make of the two qualifying phrases, literally "in/by flesh" and "in/by spirit"? The NIV correctly reflects the fact that a literal rendering of these into English would be meaningless to a modern reader. The translators considered what Peter intended to convey in the two phrases and decided that Christ was put to death *in the body* and made alive *by the Spirit*. Other interpretations are possible (see the alternative translations *in the spirit* in the NIV margin and the note below).

The first phrase means in any case that Jesus died a physical death. "Flesh" can stand for our physical nature generally (compare 2:11). The phrase indicates as plainly as could be that Jesus was a real, physical human being and that he died the same kind of death that we all have

---

the quickening of his soul to visit the underworld before his resurrection on the third day. But this is not very probable, because either we must regard the soul of Jesus as immortal (in which case no "making alive" was necessary) or as being mortal and brought to life (in which case it was treated like the soul of any other human being and it is difficult to see why the point should have been mentioned at all). The latter interpretation is also faulty because it suggests that only the body of Jesus was human and only his spirit was divine, which is contrary to orthodox understanding of Jesus as being one person.

2.°More commonly "flesh" and "spirit" are thought of as representing two spheres of being or manners of existence. Christ died in that he belonged to the sphere of physical life, but he was raised to life in that he belonged to (or entered) the sphere of spiritual life. This is the way in which NIV takes the same phrase ten verses later (4:6; compare Rom 1:3; 1 Tim 3:16).

to die.

The second phrase, as interpreted by the NIV, states that he was brought to life by the activity of the Spirit of God, whose function in bringing resurrection life to mortal bodies is attested elsewhere in the New Testament (Rom 1:4; 8:11; the first reference associates the Spirit with the appointment of Jesus as Son of God with power at his resurrection). From what Paul says in 1 Corinthians 15 we know that he believed that the physical body of Jesus was transformed into a spiritual body. We do not know whether Peter shared this belief, but what he teaches here is at least in harmony with it. Although Peter does not explicitly say so, he may well be implying that when Christ "brings" Christians "to God," they are resurrected in the same way as he was.

Christ's Proclamation to the Spirits (3:19-20) We now come to the most tricky part of this section. Its central affirmation is that Christ went and preached to the spirits in prison, who are identified as those who disobeyed long ago in the days of Noah.

This is a real problem for the expositor. It is a good rule that congregations should not be presented with a variety of interpretations, which can cause confusion. This passage is open to different interpretations, and it is not easy to explain them or to show why one view is preferable to another. The wisest course is to admit that the details of the passage are heavily disputed, to present one view (or at most two) and to avoid making any applications that are dubiously based.

I will begin by stating the three main interpretations of the passage and then compare them in detail. Although the view designated as 1b appears to me the most probable, I recognize that any conclusion must be tentative.

1. Christ went to the place where disobedient supernatural powers are

---

3:19 It may be helpful to indicate which recent commentators adopt the various interpretations. For view 1a, see Selwyn (1947); Stibbs (1959); Best (1971); for view 1b, see Dalton (1965); Kelly (1969); France (1977); Michaels (1988). For view 2, see Goppelt (1978). View 3, which goes back to Augustine, has been given fresh life by Feinberg (1986) and Grudem (1988:203-39; compare Clowney 1988:162-64).

Through whom interprets the Greek "in which" as a reference to the Spirit. But this is a most odd way to express this thought. If the reference is to the realm of the Spirit, then we may interpret the phrase to mean "alive in the Spirit, through which" (as in NIV margin) or, preferably, "in which spiritual mode of existence." Another possibility is that the Greek phrase functions as a conjunction: "in the course of which [process of dying and rising]."

imprisoned. This is variously taken to refer to a journey (a) "down" to Hades before his resurrection or (b) "up" to a prison in the heavens after his resurrection. In either place he proclaimed to them his victory and God's judgment. On this view the incident is mentioned primarily to assure the readers that Christ is superior to all powers and that believers have no need to fear them.

2. Christ went to Hades (as in 1a) and preached to the spirits of the people who were disobedient in Noah's day. For some commentators (a) this was simply an announcement of victory and judgment (as in view 1); for others (b) it was a proclamation of the gospel, giving them a "second chance" in their postmortem state.

3. Christ entered into Noah and through him preached to those who were disobedient during the building of the ark. He preached the need for repentance, but the people refused to listen (only Noah's family being saved). They perished in the flood, and their spirits are now in prison. Thus Christ in Noah is an example and encouragement to Peter's readers to preach the gospel fearlessly.

We can now tackle the main questions raised by the passage:

□ **When did Christ go?** The most commonly accepted view is that the event described in this passage took place at the time of the death and resurrection of Christ. He performed the task in the Spirit before he finally went into heaven (3:22). There are, however, two possibilities. The older interpretation (views 1a and 2) posits that between Good Friday and Easter Sunday, Christ descended into the temporary abode of the dead (Hades not hell), where disobedient spirits are imprisoned, to make his proclamation. The more recent interpretation (view 1b) is that Peter is referring to a visit made by Jesus after his resurrection in connection with his ascension to the right hand of God in heaven. Christ

---

The majority of attempts to correct the text of the New Testament without textual evidence are best forgotten. Maybe we should simply forget the conjecture that after the conjunction *(en hoi kai)* the word "Enoch" was dropped out of the text. On this view, it was not Christ but Enoch who visited the spirits in prison. The conjecture is unnecessary and wrong, but nevertheless interesting because it points us to the background of thought in the verse. By the first century there existed a number of legends about the patriarch Enoch, whose remarkable departure from the world (Gen 5:24) was the stimulus for suggesting that he travelled to places visited by no other man. In 1 Enoch much is made of the "sons of God" of Gen 6:1-4 as fallen angelic beings who sinned with humankind. These "Watchers" were therefore condemned to imprisonment:

visited the prison of disobedient spirits that is situated in the heavens.

Over against this view is the suggestion (view 3) that the passage refers to Christ's preaching in and through Noah to the latter's contemporaries. The spirit of Christ was active in Noah, as it was in the prophets (1:11), and empowered him to be a preacher of righteousness (2 Pet 2:5). A final decision between these views can be made only in the light of other details in the passage. View 3 has in its favor the parallel of Christ/Noah and Peter's readers as fearless preachers to hostile audiences. It also preserves continuity between the references to the flood and baptism. Second Corinthians 13:3 demonstrates that the idea of Christ speaking in somebody is not impossible.

View 3 faces insuperable difficulties. The passage most naturally refers to an incident that took place after Christ had been *made alive*. The spirit of Christ inspiring the prophets is not the same thing as Christ himself going and acting in Noah, and there are no other parallels to Christ temporarily inhabiting Old Testament characters. Above all, this view requires a double reinterpretation of verse 19. After having read it once in terms of the spirits and Christ, the readers must then reinterpret *the spirits in prison* as the people in Noah's day (see below) and *he* as "he in the person of Noah." The major weakness of this view is that Noah is not named as the one through whom Christ preached.

□ *Where did Christ go?* If we must decide between views 1a and 1b, several considerations are relevant.

On 1a: The belief that the abode of the dead is under the earth is found in the Old Testament, which speaks of going down to Sheol (Ps 30:3; Is 14:15; compare Lk 10:15), and in Revelation 20:1-3, where the prison of Satan is in the abyss. Jesus is said to have been in Hades (Mt 12:40; Acts 2:27, 31), but it is not said that he preached there (Mt 16:18;

Bind them for seventy generations underneath the rocks of the ground until the day of their judgment and of their consummation until the eternal judgment is concluded. In those days they will lead them into the bottom of the fire—and in torment—in the prison [where] they will be locked up for ever. (1 Enoch 10:12-13)

Enoch was sent to visit them and tell them that there was no hope for them:

And they said to me, "Enoch, scribe of righteousness, go and make known to the Watchers of heaven who have abandoned the high heaven, the holy eternal place, and have defiled themselves with women, as their deeds move the children of the world, and have taken unto themselves wives." (1 Enoch 12:4)

In 1 Enoch the place of imprisonment appears to be beneath the ground. However, in 2

Rom 10:7; Eph 4:8-10; and Rev 1:18 must be understood otherwise). On this view the spirit of Jesus was active while it was separated from his body.

On 1b: The Jews believed that there were several levels or divisions in heaven, a view shared by Paul, who relates how "a man in Christ" ascended to the third heaven (2 Cor 12:2). Some Jewish writings locate the place where the evil powers are kept in subjection until the final judgment in one of these divisions of heaven. We may observe how Satan himself is in heaven until he is thrown down to the earth (Rev 12:7). So it is possible that the reference here is to a visit paid by the resurrected Jesus to a prison in heaven. (There was a story that Enoch visited and toured the heavens. *See note below.*)

The ideas that the spirits were imprisoned down below or up above were both current. R. T. France points out that the text says nothing about Christ going down, and that the event took place after he had been resurrected. He also argues that the abode of the dead to which Christ *went* (as in the Nicene Creed) should not be confused with the prison of the spirits. If we have to choose between these two possibilities, the latter has the better case.

□ *To whom did Christ go?* Again we have to deal with the three different interpretations:

1. The *spirits* are evil supernatural beings. The word "spirits" can certainly be used in this sense, both of angels (Heb 1:14; 12:9; Acts 23:8-9) and evil beings (Mk 1:23; Lk 10:20; Acts 19:15-16). The story of the "fallen angels" who seduced mankind in the days before the flood (Gen 6:1-4) was a popular one in New Testament times. Furthermore, the story of their being kept in prison until the day of judgment was well known (2 Pet 2:4; Jude 6).

Enoch 7 and in Testament of Levi 3:2 the place is in heaven and is visited by Enoch. Clearly various, literally incompatible views were current.

Grudem tries hard to show that the sons of God in Genesis 6 were not necessarily regarded as angelic powers and that the angels did not necessarily sin specifically at the time of the flood, but his case is unconvincing. The most that he can do is to show that other opinions existed in Judaism. He cannot deny the existence of the opinion that he attempts to play down.

Prison is the traditional understanding of Greek *phylakē* here. Michaels's suggestion (1988:206-9) that the word means "a refuge" is very dubious. He offers it largely because the spirits are still active rather than restrained. But this overlooks the possibility that only

2. Christ preached to the spirits of dead people, kept in the abode of the dead until the last judgment. More commonly we would speak of the "souls" of the dead, but the word "spirit" can be used in this sense (Num 16:22; 27:16; Heb 12:23). The thought that they are in prison is found in early Christian writings. Because the contemporaries of Noah, who spurned God, were proverbial for extreme wickedness, we can readily understand that they represent the wicked in general.

3. If Christ preached in the person of Noah, then *spirits in prison* describes the human beings who were disobedient during the building of the ark.

Let us now assess these different interpretations:

In favor of view 2, some scholars note that when New Testament authors use the word "spirits" to denote spirits of dead persons, it is always qualified in such a way as to make this clear. They then claim the description in verse 20 of the disobedience of the spirits to whom Christ preached fits human rather than supernatural beings.

There is, of course, no dispute that humankind sinned at the time of the flood. The period just before the flood had become proverbial in Judaism for disbelief and indifference to God (Lk 17:26-27). The wickedness of those opposed to God was seen as all the more culpable because this was the time when God patiently waited for sinners to repent and through Noah proclaimed righteousness to them (2 Pet 2:5).

Noah's construction of the ark should have made them turn to God. Here was a remarkable sign, a man aided by a few members of his family building a vast boat on dry land, far from the sea, because he had been warned about a coming flood, but they did not pay heed to the warning. "Disobey" is essentially the same as "disbelieve." In the end only eight

---

one group of spirits is under restraint while others are still active.

3:20 A major argument advanced by Grudem for view 3 is that this verse should be translated not as he "preached to the spirits in prison who disobeyed long ago when God waited patiently," but rather as he "preached to the spirits in prison when they disobeyed long ago when God waited patiently." The difference is that on the latter translation the preaching and the disobeying were simultaneous, whereas on the usual view the disobedience preceded the preaching.

Grudem argues that the participle used without an article after the noun demands this sense. But this is not correct. First, as Grudem admits, the force of the participle is ambiguous. It could be causal or temporal. If it is temporal, it could equally well be translated "when or after they had formerly disobeyed." Since the participle is aorist rather than

people went into the ark and were delivered from the flood. Scarcely could a more potent indicator be found as to how deliberately Noah's contemporaries had turned away from God.

However, it is not certain that verse 20 implies that God was patiently waiting for the spirits of these disobedient persons to repent. In the last part of the verse the focus shifts to the human beings who actually were saved. The spirits may be regarded rather as preventing other human beings from responding to God's patience. The spirits are not unambiguously identified as human beings.

Further, it is unprecedented to speak of the spirits of the dead being kept in *prison*. It may also be significant that when Peter speaks of the eight people being saved, he uses the word *psychē* rather than *pneuma* (see note).

There are also strong arguments against view 3. First, it is not clear why Peter would describe human spirits so unusually, in terms of their present imprisonment rather than their perishing in the flood.

A second point is that the reader is required to interpret *spirits* as "the beings who are now spirits but were then men and women." Proponents of this view urge that the same phenomenon occurs in 4:6, where the gospel was preached *also to the dead*—that is, "to people who are now dead but were then alive." A sufficient rebuttal of this parallel, however, is to point out that the odd use of *the dead* there is necessitated by the reference in 4:5. Peter is concerned with how people now dead will be ultimately judged, whether by human or divine standards. The two cases are not parallel.

It follows that view 1 is the least difficult. It corresponds to Peter's reference to evil powers in 3:22. *Angels, authorities and powers* hangs

present, this translation is the more probable, since the aorist participle usually (though not always) expresses an action preceding the time of the main verb. Most of Grudem's parallels have present participles. Second, the use of *pote* ("at one time, long ago") with the participle, rather than the main verb, is most peculiar; it more naturally suggests a contrast in time between the disobeying and the preaching.

Another possibility regarding the disobedience of the spirits is that Peter may have had in mind the "Nephilim," or giants, who were the offspring of the disobedient angelic beings and human women, or that under "spirits" he includes both the fallen angels and humankind.

Through water could possibly mean that they were saved *by* means of the water which bore up the ark. Although this gives a smooth connection with the next verse, it is rather too sophisticated an interpretation.

on its own if not related to the spirits.

□ *What did Christ preach?* Advocates of views 2b and 3 note that the Greek verb is normally used of preaching the gospel. Some defenders of view 2b have argued that Christ preached the gospel to the souls of the flood generation, giving them, in effect, a second chance of repentance. Those who take this view then tend to argue that this group of the dead represents all the dead (on the principle that if even the worst sinners are given a second chance, so too are the rest of the dead). Although this verse says nothing about the result of the preaching, some suggest that all who get this second chance will respond to it and be saved. They corroborate this conclusion with 4:6, which they interpret to mean that the gospel was preached to the dead so that they might "live in the spirit"—that is, "be saved."

There are various objections to this universalist view. It is certainly not a necessary interpretation of the passage. The verb "preach" can mean no more than "make proclamation" (Rev 5:2; compare Jn 1:2; 3:2, 4), in contrast with the verb "to preach the gospel" in 4:6. Furthermore, 4:6 is most plausibly interpreted otherwise (see below). Above all, it is not clear what the point of the statement would be, unless it is to say that just as Christ preached the gospel to the worst of sinners, so Christians must be prepared to witness to their persecutors (supporting 3:15).

Much more likely is the view that Christ made proclamation to the evil powers, announcing his victory on the cross and confirming their defeat. They are now subject to him (3:22) and those who are persecuted need not be afraid of the evil spiritual powers who inspire their persecutors. Christ is Lord! Hallelujah!

If we interpret the passage in this way (view 1b), we see that Peter aimed to present Christ as an example of suffering for doing good, to show how his death brings believers to God, to stress the fact that though Christ died he was brought to life (as believers will be), to emphasize how Christ proclaimed his triumph to the spirits who corrupted the people of Noah's time, and to stress that Christ, now enthroned alongside God, is superior to all supernatural powers. Consequently, Christians can confidently stand up to hostility and bear a courageous witness (4:1-6), knowing that they will be vindicated just as Christ was.

□ *The Symbol and the Reality* Before proceeding further with exposition of the passage we must pause to ask about the significance of what we have discovered. What exactly is Peter doing here? He knows that Christ did something during the period of his death and resurrection, but how did Peter come to know and to express it in this way? Some say that Peter has expressed his point in mythological language. He is writing about a sphere of which he had no direct knowledge; therefore, he had to use existing imagery to convey his meaning to his readers. We note that what Peter says about Christ in some ways parallels what Jewish tradition said about Enoch, so that Enoch is the type to which Christ is the antitype. Peter appears to have expressed the significance of Jesus' death and resurrection by using imagery and language drawn from the Enoch story to depict dramatically Christ's victory over all of the powers of evil. This way of presenting things may have come to Peter either by direct revelation or by meditation on the available scriptural and extracanonical materials. Either way, of course, the Spirit of God was active in the process, whether granting direct knowledge or working concursively with Peter's mental processes. The interpretation may have been expressed here using concepts drawn from mythology, but it is nonetheless the true interpretation of the effects of the work of Christ in the spiritual realm. How should we understand what Peter says? As we have seen, there are two different interpretations of where Christ visited, somewhere "down" beneath the earth or somewhere "up" in heaven. Both directions should surely be understood metaphorically. We are speaking about spirits in any case, and they cannot be localized in the center of the earth any more than God can be localized in a heaven above the sky. Maybe it doesn't matter if we aren't certain where Christ *went.* Either way, Peter means that God's power restrained the powers of evil, that this power was expressed in the death and resurrection of Jesus and that, because of God's omnipotence, Christians need not be afraid of persecution or the evil powers that promote it.

The Significance of Christian Baptism (3:21-22) It now becomes clear why Peter introduced the disobedient spirits and the flood narrative. At the end of verse 20 he comments that, in contrast to the mass of the disobedient, only a few people were saved in the ark. He adds that they were *saved through water,* which probably means that they were brought safely through the flood because they were in the ark, without which they would have drowned.

This idea enables Peter to draw a further lesson by making a parallel between Noah's family and his readers. He uses the word "antitype" (translated by the NIV with the verb *symbolizes*) to show the parallel between the events and people at the time of the flood and the events and people in his own time. The people in the ark correspond to Christians; the water of the flood corresponds to the water of baptism; the escape of Noah's family from drowning corresponds to the spiritual salvation of believers. This Old Testament example is an actual saving event by God, which is now repeated in a new way in the case of Christians.

Whatever the precise construction, Peter says that Christian baptism saves Christians (see note). He clearly does not mean this in any material sense, as if an outward rite could convey spiritual salvation; or in any magical sense, as if the water possessed some spiritual power; or in any automatic way, so that anybody who is baptized is saved. We should not make the mistake of limiting the significance of *baptism* to the precise moment and action of being immersed or sprinkled with water. Rather, for Peter, the word "baptism" symbolically represents the whole process by which the gospel comes to people and they accept it in faith.

It is this last point which Peter emphasizes. He reminds his readers that baptism is not to be equated with the removal of dirt from the body. This protest against mere outward washing was necessary in a society

---

3:21 NIV adopts the most obvious interpretation of the antecedent of the Greek relative pronoun and takes it to refer to the water (literally, "saved through water; which [water] also saves you"). This translation assumes that the word "antitype" refers to the way in which the water symbolizes baptism. This is difficult if we do not take *through water* as the means of saving Noah's family in verse 20. Alternatively we may interpret it: "and, as an antitype to the whole event, baptism now saves you" or "which [water], namely, baptism, now saves you who are the antitype of Noah's family." The meaning is not greatly affected.

The interpretation of this verse has been plagued by Protestant fear of finding in it a basis for the doctrine of "baptismal regeneration." This view ties the experience of receiving the Spirit and being regenerated to the moment of baptism with water and sees this experience as taking place regardless of the repentance and faith of the person baptized. In the Anglican *Book of Common Prayer,* for example, after an infant has been baptized we find the words, "Seeing now . . . that this child is regenerate."

There is no justification for this view in Scripture. What Peter is talking about is the occasion when a person comes to water-baptism seeking salvation through faith in Jesus Christ. "Baptism saves you" is simply a shorthand way of saying, "God saves you in and through the act of baptism, which is the outward expression of the twin facts that he

that was only gradually realizing that outward defilement was not spiritually significant—that is, outward removal of dirt or contamination due
to contact with sinners is not the same thing as inward spiritual renewal.
Still today, of course, people think that outward acts like coming to
church and receiving communion somehow make them acceptable to
God even if their hearts are guilty of evil. It is curious how people who
rarely attend church still want baptism of their infants, church weddings
and Christian funerals. Peter's attitude rejects all such ideas in principle.

On the contrary, baptism must represent or express *the pledge of a
good conscience toward God*. The translation in the NIV text suggests
either that we come to baptism with a good conscience (the marginal
note, *the response of a good conscience*, offers much the same sense),
or that we pledge ourselves to maintain a good conscience by not sinning. The former of these possibilities is unlikely. We come to baptism
not because we have a good conscience—one that does not accuse us
of having done wrong—but precisely because we feel guilty and in need
of forgiveness and renewal. We should either adopt the latter possibility—namely, that the pledge is one to break with sin for the future—or
side with those commentators who take the Greek word to mean an
"appeal" or "petition" to God for a good conscience. It is thus a prayer
for forgiveness and cleansing.

Baptism saves us not by any virtue in itself but by the effects of Jesus'
resurrection. The significance of this fact is brought out in verse 22,

---

regenerates you by his Spirit on the basis of the atonement wrought by Christ and that you
come committing yourself in faith and repentance to Christ as your Savior." Needless to say,
evangelical Anglicans hold that the language of their baptismal service should not be interpreted in terms of baptismal regeneration.

The word translated "pledge" *(eperōtēma)* can mean "question" or "request" or it can
refer to the clause containing a formal question and answer in a contract. Hence it can refer
to the actual reply or legal pledge in the contract.

3:22 The picture here is ultimately derived from the messianic exaltation of Psalm 110:1.
Few verses in the Old Testament are alluded to so frequently in the New Testament. Peter
emphasizes that Jesus *has gone* into heaven, thus speaking of his ascension, which is implicit
in talk of his exaltation. It is, therefore, incorrect to suggest that the tradition of the ascension
is peculiar to Luke and not found elsewhere in the New Testament (see 1 Tim 3:16). The
thought of the subordination of the hostile powers is also found in Psalm 110:1. Peter refers
to the hostile powers as (fallen) *angels, authorities and powers;* similar terms are used by
Paul (Rom 8:38; 1 Cor 15:24; Col 1:16; 2:10, 15; Eph 1:21; 3:10; 6:12). The variety of terms
strongly suggests that it would be wrong to try to identify different classes of powers in terms
of this vocabulary or to create a consistent picture.

which reminds us that the risen Jesus is in fact the exalted Jesus who occupies the seat of power beside God and is superior to all the hostile powers.

By what he says in verses 21-22 Peter has made three things clear. First, just as Noah and his family escaped despite the disobedience of the evil spirits in their day, so too Christians will be saved and not be overcome by the evil forces behind persecution. Salvation is not just from sin but also from the powers that threaten us and our salvation. In fact, nothing "in all creation will be able to separate us from the love of God" (Rom 8:38).

Second, although baptism is the normal means of Christian initiation, salvation is not the result of merely submitting outwardly to baptism. It is for those who come to God with a longing to be set free from sin and to have a pure conscience.

Third, the one source of spiritual victory is the crucified and risen Jesus. Peter concludes the section with encouragement for the persecuted: "Do not be afraid. The Christ whom you accept as your Lord truly is Lord over all the opposition that you may face."

Maintaining a Christian Lifestyle (4:1-6) Stores that sell things to wear no longer advertise them as "clothes" but as "fashions." And though the very name indicates how short-lived any particular style of clothing is, it encourages us to purchase the latest, most up-to-date apparel so that we will not fall out of step with the perceived majority (or at least the trendsetters). We don't want to look old-fashioned, odd or as if we are unable to afford to live in style.

What is true of clothes is true of habits. Smoking is advertised as the "adult" thing to teen-agers, so that they will start the habit young. Once they are "hooked," they won't ask whether or not it is fashionable. The consumption of alcohol is similarly pushed as the "in" thing for everybody. So much so that even Christians, whose traditions have warned them against use of a drug (some would call it a poison) with an appalling record for stimulating crime, danger on the roads and disease,

Notes: **4:1** The phrase *arm yourselves* brings out the force of the Greek, which conveys the metaphor of going out to battle after putting on armor. If we put on or adopt the same frame of mind as Jesus had, we shall find that we have protected ourselves against the attacks of temptation.

The interpretation of the final clause is debated: (1) The person who is prepared to

are lured by the trend.

One might suppose that Christians living in a hostile environment would want to shun all that reeks of paganism, but in practice things are not so simple. In the first place, everyone of us is weak and attracted by what the writer to the Hebrews realistically calls "the pleasures of sin" (Heb 11:25). Even though we know that certain activities are wrong, we are still attracted by the element of pleasure that they contain. In a weak moment we are prepared to disobey.

Second, we can have genuine uncertainty as to whether a particular activity is right or wrong (and whether earlier generations made the right decisions in "gray areas") or as to where we draw the line. For example, is the use of alcohol and other potentially addictive drugs for other than medicinal reasons (1 Tim 5:23) allowable for Christians? If it is, where do you stop?

Third, we know that Christ prayed for us to remain "in the world." We must not cut ourselves off from the very people to whom we are trying to bear Christian witness. How do we keep in touch with a pleasure-loving, affluent society? And finally, we are all tempted to conform in order to avoid being thought of as killjoys by other people.

To these kinds of struggles Peter addresses himself in this section. He asserts that, despite the pressures of society, Christians should live as the people of God, following the example of Christ. He stresses in various ways that his readers must regard themselves as being done with sinful pleasures, which will lead in the end to divine judgment.

Suffering or Sinning (4:1) Peter begins by drawing a lesson from what he said just previously about Christ's suffering. He now uses Christ as an example that Christians must follow. His point is essentially that a person who suffers shows that he has given up those things against which his suffering is a protest. In other words, by suffering Christ showed his opposition to sinful living. Therefore, persecuted Christians must follow his example and say a firm no to their temptations. The thought is rather condensed, and verse one can be paraphrased more

undergo unjust suffering shows that he holds firmly to a principle, in this case, opposition to and refusal to sin; (2) the person who has died—that is, with Christ in his baptism (as in Rom 6:1-7)—has died to sin and thus ceased from sinning; (3) the person who is persecuted is purified from sin by his sufferings; (4) since it is death that brings the sinful flesh to an end, the Christian must be prepared to suffer death just as Christ did (the person

fully like this:

> Persons who are prepared to suffer demonstrate that they have a particular attitude toward certain principles. Jesus was prepared to suffer, and therefore he must have had this attitude. Since you have been called to suffer like Jesus did (3:14-18), you should also adopt the same attitude as he had. (It would be foolish merely to suffer without holding the principles which his sufferings demonstrated that he held.) You will find that this attitude acts like armor in protecting you from temptation. For the particular attitude which Christ had is related to sin. It can be summed up in the saying: A person who suffers in the flesh has ceased from sin.

Two Ways of Living (4:2-4) Peter next points out that there are two opposing ways of life for the Christian to choose. The first of them, which is inconsistent with the very nature of being a Christian, is to live in accordance with the desires of human beings. Here Peter is plainly thinking of "human" in the sense of "fallen human." Again, though the word "desires" can refer to good or bad desires (Phil 1:23; 1 Thess 2:17), the qualifying adjective shows that Peter intends "sinful desires" (as in 2:11). The word translated "not" is literally "no longer," and brings out the fact, expressed even more clearly in verse 3, that all Christians were controlled by sinful desires in the past, but must *no longer* be so controlled for the future.

The second way of life conforms to the will of God. Elsewhere when Peter uses this phrase, he means the divine purpose that may involve suffering for his people (3:17; 4:19), but he can also mean the divine purpose that his people should do good (2:15). But the meaning is so obvious that he does not spell it out in detail here.

---

who has this "insight" and who willingly bears persecution is already committed to dying to the flesh in principle); (5) the person who has died is Christ; in dying he has finished with the sin that he was bearing for others and put it behind him (Michaels 1988:225-9).

View 3 can be quickly set aside. View 5 is far from self-evident. The problem is, then, whether Peter is stating a psychological truth (1) or a spiritual fact (2 or 4). View 2 is unlikely to be the right one, for although Peter's theology has close affinities with Paul's, the word used here is "suffer," not "die," and the thought is of suffering persecution, not of spiritual death. View 4 is too overly subtle. View 1 remains the most likely, though it is, of course, stated as an ideal and not as a universally true fact.

The emphasis on *the body* (Gk "flesh") in verses 4 and 6 is important. Here Peter shares Paul's view that sin is committed by our fallen human nature. This is not to suggest that sin is purely physical and not related to the mind or heart of man. Consequently, when

Peter is concerned with the readers' use of time (v. 3). Before their conversion they had already spent quite enough time in worldly pursuits and now, almost as if to make up for the wasted years, they should refrain from previous practices—what *pagans choose to do.* The rest of their lives should be devoted to doing the will of God.

The list of sins covers the more obvious "lusts of the flesh," including:

1. *Debauchery,* or outrageous acts that offend a public sense of decency. Admittedly, the public sense is fickle and culturally relative, but such a standard does exist. Unfortunately, homosexual acts have gradually become more acceptable in Western culture, but (thank God) public decency still protests against such acts involving minors. In a limited and inadequate way the public standard reflects ultimate moral standards, and so Peter is thinking of acts by people who want to go beyond whatever is recognized as allowable and flaunt their freedom to do as they like.

2. *Lust.* Here the Greek word for "desires" appears in such evil company that its morally bad quality can be taken for granted. The word implies sexual desires of an illicit character leading to illicit acts.

3. *Drunkenness, orgies, carousing.* These are virtual synonyms for parties characterized by excessive drinking and consequent noisy and unseemly behavior.

4. *Detestable idolatry.* This refers to pagan religious cults that incorporated practices offensive to Christian sensibilities, such as excessive drinking (associated with the cult of Dionysus), eating food sacrificed to idols, offering sacrifices to idols (in contempt of the one true God), and (in some cults) ritual prostitution. Today many of these practices have been divorced from idolatry, but they are still carried on in con-

---

people are prepared to say no to their human nature by submitting voluntarily to the pain of persecution, they show most clearly that they are opposed to seeking the pleasures of sin enjoyed by their human nature.

4:3 The reference to pagan pursuits need not imply that the readers were all former pagans. Jews too were quite capable of falling into such sins. The point is rather that these were the kind of practices one might expect from people without any knowledge of God, whereas the Jews should know better. It is worth recording that the Greek philosopher Epicurus, so commonly regarded as promoting an ethic of sheer pleasure, expressly stated that he advocated the pleasures of the mind and not the pleasures of the body, such as eating and drinking.

Detestable renders the Greek *athemitos;* the other sense of the word, "lawless," is inappropriate here.

tempt of God. The argument that some activities were condemned primarily because they were associated with idolatry is scarcely a warrant for assuming that the activities in themselves are morally and spiritually neutral. While evil in themselves, they are all the more evil as lifestyles that want to have nothing to do with God.

If Christians abstain from these things, their former associates will be surprised and shocked at their change of lifestyle (v. 4). To be sure, the old way of life can be characterized from a Christian point of view—and even by the standards of pagan moralists—as plunging madly into a veritable flood of dissipation. But people are often prepared to make allowances for occasional indulgence ("just this once") without condemning human desires absolutely. Peter was not so tolerant.

But there is more to it than surprise and shock. If Christians take a firm and consistent stand against this way of life, then by implication they condemn their former associates. So the "pagans" attack and *heap abuse* on Christians. The Greek word means "to slander" or perhaps even "to blaspheme," and may convey the idea that they blaspheme the God whom Christians obey (v. 2). Although Peter writes in these verses about people who go to obvious excess in bodily indulgence, it is worth asking a few questions. The first concerns the rationale of his attack on this way of life: Why is it contrary to the will of God for Christians? Two others concern application: Does what he says need to be adapted in any way to the modern situation? Does his principle extend to other lifestyles not mentioned?

4:5 For the judgment of the living and the dead, see Acts 10:42 and 2 Timothy 4:1. Peter does not indicate clearly whether the judgment is carried out by God the Father (1:17; 2:23; Rom 14:10) or by Christ (Acts 10:42; 1 Cor 4:4-5; 2 Cor 5:10). In 2 Timothy 4:1, God and Christ are associated in judgment and, in John 5:27, the Father gives the authority to judge to the Son. However, since Peter normally refers to God as judge, this is probably the reference here.

4:6 This verse has raised almost as many problems as 3:19. Much of the difficulty lies in determining whether the two verses refer to the same thing.

1. A common view of the two verses is that both of them refer to the preaching by Christ in the abode of the dead. And whereas 3:19 singles out the especially wicked people of Noah's time (and could thereby be taken to imply that other, less wicked people also heard the message), 4:6 refers to a universal proclamation to the dead. To the universal judgment in verse 5 corresponds a universal proclamation of the gospel giving people the opportunity to respond to Christ even after they have died.

The arguments in favor of this view are the apparent parallelism with 3:19, the repetition of the flesh/spirit antithesis from 3:18 and the suggestion that the word "dead" implies that

1. The objections to idolatry and godless living need no further justification from a Christian point of view. A way of life which fails to honor God, whether motivated by the belief in no god or the worship of other gods, is obviously wrong. The honoring or placing of any thing or person above or alongside of God is the sin of idolatry.

2. The various sins of the flesh are wrong not merely because they may be connected with idol worship but, above all, because they express a misuse of the human body. For example, promiscuous sexual relationships not only threaten a marriage but open a person up to infection by sexually transmitted diseases. Again, drugs take away a person's self-control and sobriety. And though many people say that an occasional loss of self-control is a good and pleasurable experience, even an isolated instance of adultery is still adultery—and still sin.

3. The flouting of public decency clearly indicates a natural human consciousness of "going too far." By what criteria should these limits be fixed? Of course, God's desire is that all his creatures should enjoy the blessings that he created for them. What is wrong is the selfish and sinful indulgence of our desires for pleasure. The sins condemned here consist in indulgence of self despite the consequences for other people and despite the spiritual cost. Worldly behavior in general consists in self-indulgence of any kind at the cost of others.

The Significance of the Judgment (4:5-6) Whatever be the human verdict on such a way of life, it stands under divine judgment. Those who practice it and who abuse Christians for failing to live the same way

the people in question were already dead when they heard the proclamation.

However, the insuperable obstacle to this view is that it does not explain what the function of the verse is in its context. The point of verse 5 is that persecutors will be condemned at the judgment. A statement that the dead will hear the gospel and live follows on most illogically from this. The reference can hardly be to Peter's readers since they are people who believed in the gospel while still alive in the body.

2. The view that the dead in verse 6 means the *spiritually* dead who hear the gospel in this life obviates the difficulty of view 1 above, and can be supported by biblical usage elsewhere (Lk 9:59-60; Jn 5:25; Eph 2:1, 5). But a jump from the literally dead in verse 5 to the spiritually dead in verse 6 is unlikely, and again the verse seems unmotivated in its context.

3. The best view, therefore, is that the reference is to Christians who are now dead but who heard and responded to the gospel before they died. The apparently strange use of the term "dead" to signify "people who subsequently died" is fully explained by the need to make a connection with the use of the word in verse 5. Possibly Peter has martyrs in mind—people who were regarded as proved wrong by their persecutors but who would

may seem to have the upper hand for the time being, but the last word will be with God. He is already prepared to judge every person, both living and dead. A time will come when world history will stop and God will intervene to judge the world. Those who are still alive will face God, and those who have died will be raised up to answer for themselves before God.

Because there will be a final judgment, what the world thinks of Christians does not matter. What matters is the twofold fact that the pagans will have to answer to God for their refusal to obey him and that those who heard and believed the gospel will be vindicated by God and enjoy eternal life. Christians may have been condemned while they were still in the body—their physical death may have been regarded as evidence of their condemnation—but in accordance with God's standard of judgment they will enjoy life in the realm of the Spirit. This future life is theirs because the gospel was preached to them and they responded to it.

Thus Peter has drawn the contrast between pagan and Christian lifestyles, and he has shown that Christians must be prepared to suffer rather than revert to the lifestyle that they followed before their conversion. This is not an easy message for Christians to proclaim in the world today with its firm belief that physical death is the end and that one should conduct a way of life within that horizon. But plenty of educated people in the ancient world believed just that, and so Peter's message does not really require translation for today.

In addition to the fact of future judgment we need to stress the reality

---

be vindicated by God. Michaels suggests that "the righteous of Israel's past" are included in the reference (1988:237). The thought is closely paralleled in the Jewish understanding of martyrdom in Wisdom:

> But the souls of the righteous are in the hand of God, and no torment will ever touch them. In the eyes of the foolish they seemed to have died, and their departure was thought to be an affliction, and their going from us to be their destruction; but they are at peace. For though in the sight of men they were punished, their hope is full of immortality. Having been disciplined a little, they will receive great good, because God tested them and found them worthy of himself; like gold in the furnace he tried them, and like a sacrificial burnt offering he accepted them. (3:1-6)

The echoes of this passage in 1 Peter 1:6-7 strongly suggest that Peter was familiar with this line of thought.

The one real objection to this view is the suggestion that it is unnatural to take "the gospel was preached to the dead" in the sense "the gospel was preached [in their lifetime] to those

of God's opposition to worldly, dissolute behavior and to demonstrate that such a lifestyle contains the seeds of its own destruction, both for those who practice it and for those who are harmed by their actions. It is precisely this latter idea that today's permissive society refuses to believe. How much more necessary, then, that Christians recognize it and testify to it as compellingly and as urgently as possible.

The Life of the Christian Congregation (4:7-11) In recent years the loyalty that is essential for the successful running of government offices has been sharply threatened by the treachery of so-called moles, persons who have access to state secrets and who are prepared to reveal them to the public. Regardless of the moral arguments affecting ultimate loyalty, whether to senior government officials or to the interests of the public generally, clearly loyalty and unity are essential if a government would stand firm against rivals and opposition.

Similarly, in the church where there is a lack of love and common purpose and where the spiritual lifeline of communication to God is broken, the forces of opposition will weaken and eventually destroy the church. Paul's letter to the church at Philippi makes it clear that the congregation was facing attacks from outside itself and that these attacks were a much greater danger than they might otherwise have been because church members were not fully united and showing love and mutual care (1:27-28). Paul had to urge them to be of one mind (2:1-4), and he even mentioned by name specific people who had fallen out with one another and needed to be reconciled (4:2).

---

who [having subsequently died] are now dead." In its favor is that only on this view does the verse make sense in the context. It draws the required contrast between the fate of persecutors and those whom they persecute. Those who judged others in their lifetime will one day be judged themselves; those who were judged and condemned in their lifetime will be upheld by God at the final judgment. It goes without saying that Peter has in mind people who not only heard the gospel but also *responded to it with faith.*

The phrase *according to God* may mean that they live in accordance with God's favorable judgment on them. Other possibilities are that they live according to the image or likeness of God or that they live in accordance with the power of God who gives them life. The parallelism with *according to men* supports the first interpretation.

In regard to the spirit must refer to the sphere of spiritual life in the next world, just as Christ came to life again in that sphere. It is unlikely to mean that those who were once "spiritually dead" now live in the Spirit in this world, a sentiment, of course, found elsewhere (Eph 2:1-6).

Peter has in mind this same kind of situation as he continues to encourage and strengthen churches that faced external opposition. In these verses he emphasizes how crucial it is that local churches be strong in fellowship with firm links of love and loyalty between the members and also between the members and God.

The End of the Age (4:7) All this applies even more strongly in the situation summed up in the phrase *the end of all things is near.* Peter has just commented on the reality of judgment for the persecutors of the church (also for the church itself; see 4:17). He now reminds his readers that this judgment is not so far distant. It is one of the events that is associated with the End—that is, the dissolution of the present world-order with the final intervention of God in history to set up his own rule in the new world.

Associated with the concept of the end of the world was the general belief that it would be immediately preceded by a time of increasing persecution of God's people as the forces of evil engaged in "one last fling" before their final doom. That is why we have the pictures of fearful conditions in the teaching of Jesus in Mark 13 and similar passages, especially in Revelation.

To be sure, the early Christians had to be warned against trying to calculate the date of the End from the events surrounding them. What they could be sure of was that the End was near, but how near was not to be a matter for speculation. Hence Peter's line of thought here is that the persecution afflicting the church should be viewed as one sign of the world's imminent end. Thus, he injects a note of urgency into Christian living. If the coming of Jesus is near, then Christians must be ready for him. Those who live lives inconsistent with their faith will experience the coming of Jesus as a dreadful shock (see 1 Thess 5:1-11).

Nevertheless, Peter did not necessarily deduce the nearness of the End from the fact of persecution. The universal Christian belief was that the End was near as a result of the coming of Jesus. The manifestation of the kingdom of God in him was the first stage in the complex event that we regard as the End of the old order. The cataclysmic event of the resurrection—and we should not underestimate how cataclysmic it was—would lead Christians to expect further events of similar and indeed greater magnitude in close connection with it.

No doubt some expected that the first stage would be followed swiftly by the next and final stages. Indeed, the end-time "horizon" of the early Christians does appear to have been understood in terms of the present generation, the next forty years or so (which are as far ahead as most people can envisage). Some Christians probably expected the return of Christ within weeks or months. It may have taken some time for them to realize that God's time-frame was more extended.

Nevertheless, the vital fact was that the coming of Jesus had inaugurated the "last days" and that from that point onwards everything must be seen in the light of the approaching End. The persecution experienced by Christians took its place as an expected sign of the End—something that would not go on indefinitely, or even successfully, but as a response by the powers of evil to the coming of Christ.

Our problem as twentieth-century Christians is twofold. First, people are unwilling in general to believe that the world can come to an end or that God can intervene in the chain of natural causes and effects. This is the familiar objection of materialists to the Christian world view as a whole. But Christians, who believe that the world is the creation of God and that God has in fact intervened in the world in the Incarnation of his Son, will not find their belief unduly strained if they claim that the same God can and will intervene again in the history of the world.

The second problem is that the lengthy passage of time since the first coming of Jesus—well beyond any forty years—calls in question the aptness of speaking of this period as "the last days" and of describing the End as "near." Does not the passage of time refute the biblical understanding of the kingdom of God? Briefly, we may claim that the biblical teaching is that God may bring the End *at any time* and that we are to live within this horizon. The writer of 2 Peter wrestled with the question and claimed that the Lord is not slow to keep his promise but that he is giving the godless every opportunity for repentance (3:8-13). This is not a solution of despair and does not take away the sense of urgency. We should also remember that, although the New Testament writers often use the future coming of Jesus as a motivation for Christian conduct, another strand in their thought teaches us that Christ is spiritually present with us always and we are, therefore, to live in a way that pleases him.

Readiness for Prayer (4:7) In this situation the priority for Christians is prayer. Peter uses the noun in the plural *prayers* to indicate that repeated acts of prayer are in his mind. But what kind of prayers? The context may well suggest that prayers in the church meeting are particularly in his mind, since the next few verses are all concerned with the congregation and its activities and relationships. The prayers themselves contribute especially to the building up of that personal relationship with Christ, which is the heart of Christian experience.

To pray in this way requires that Christians exercise a particular kind of self-discipline. The prerequisite is indicated by two verbs with roughly similar meanings. The first, *be clear minded,* carries the idea of maintaining a sense of proportion and keeping one's head despite the dangers and fears of the time. Fear and worry, stimulated by persecution, can easily lead to hasty and ill-conceived judgments. The second, *be self-controlled,* is concerned with sobriety and restraint. Coming so soon after the references to worldly carousing it probably connotes avoiding intoxication, as well as the more general sense of taking the situation seriously. It is easy to ignore unwelcome facts or to treat them with levity, and Christians are to beware of that temptation. If they have a realistic view of the world and keep alert instead of being frivolous or letting their minds be numbed by narcotics, they can turn to prayer.

A due sense of proportion should not turn Christians into killjoys or pessimists, so impressed by the sad and serious aspects of life that they are oppressed by the burden of life or continually seeking solace in prayer. This is the opposite extreme, and it is countered by the frequent New Testament teaching to be joyful in the Lord and to rejoice in the good things that he has created.

Notes: **4:7** The NIV translation omits the conjunction "but" (Gk *de*) which links this verse to what precedes. It is, no doubt, a weak conjunction, but it has the effect of turning the preceding verses (4:1-6) into a general motivation for what follows.

The phrase *is near* translates the perfect tense of a Greek verb that means "coming into a state of nearness." It can be used of things that have actually arrived or of things that once were distant but are now near. In passages like Romans 13:12-13 and James 5:8, the verb clearly must be taken in the second sense; however, in Mark 1:15, where Jesus says that the kingdom of God has drawn near, the verb refers to the actual arrival of the kingdom in his preaching, mighty works and personal presence as the Messiah.

4:8 The saying is a quotation from Proverbs 10:12, which is also found in James 5:20 and the works of some early church writers. The original saying is "Hatred stirs up contentions, but love makes a covering over all sins."

Christian Love (4:8) The second element in Peter's instruction has to do with relationships between Christians. It is introduced by *above all,* which indicates the supreme importance of love as the controlling factor in all relationships in the church (see 1:22; 2:17; 3:8). The importance of the prayer just mentioned is not disparaged. The point is that in the situation of persecution the thing that matters above all else is love toward one another. It has to be a "deep" love, but the English word doesn't adequately convey the sense of the Greek "at full stretch" (compare 1:22). Why at full stretch? Because this love will be stretched to the limit by the demands made on it. Let us remind ourselves that Christian love means caring for other people in their needs and that such care will be accompanied by a growing affection for them. Many people are prepared to care for others; they are less ready to have affection for them and to demonstrate it. It requires love at full stretch to do this.

Peter is thinking of relationships within the church, and the question of the Christian's attitude to those outside is not within his horizon at this particular point. Peter would doubtless tell us that he is concerned with the actual congregation or Christian group to which we belong. Maybe you missed the exposition of what he said about this at 1:22. Very well, let it be repeated.

There in your local church is Ann, who doesn't know much about hygiene and is frankly "smelly." Bill wears you out with incessant talking. Cathy is unspiritual. Don doesn't get along with Evelyn. Fred treats his wife badly. Gene is a gauche teen-ager, never knowing how to act with courtesy and discretion. Hilary often grumbles. Irene has a different set of interests and values (she can't come to the Tuesday-evening prayer meeting because it clashes with the local Amnesty International group).

The meaning is somewhat contested. I have taken it to mean that the person who loves overlooks the sins of the one loved. This fits with what appears to be the original sense of Proverbs 10:12 as well as with the principle in 1 Corinthians 13:5. We probably need not ask why the frequent sins of other Christians are mentioned, since we know too well how prevalent sin is among Christians, but there may be a particular relevance here in that the next verse is about hospitality. It is more difficult to put up with other people's faults in your own home than in church.

An alternative view is that God forgives the sins of the person who loves—that is, who forgives other people. This fits in with the principle stated by Jesus that it is [only] the person who forgives others who will be forgiven by God (Mt 6:14-15; Mk 11:25-26; compare Lk 7:47). The thought that God covers sins is of course biblical (Ps 32:1; 84:3), but it is not so likely to be present here where nothing in the context suggests that *God's* love is in mind.

And so on it goes. There is Kevin, to be sure, who is really quite saintly but rather drab as a person. None of them is very easy to love at full stretch. (There is also, of course, myself, and I figure in other people's lists of difficult people for similar reasons.)

And yet love is the answer to the problem. We find a whole host of offenses, real and imagined, in other people, and only love will overcome them and regard them as of no account because *love covers over a multitude of sins*. It is a verse we don't take too seriously because:

1. We think narrowly in terms of sins committed against us, when it applies to all the things in other people that irk us.

2. We tend to assume that the biblical teaching is concerned only with formal forgiveness for wrongs committed. Doubtless this is included, but the scope is wider. What Peter says here is closer to what Paul says in 1 Corinthians 13:5: "Love . . . keeps no record of wrongs." It does not treasure up the memory of wrongs committed or offenses, but releases them and does not hold them against the person. (Of course, there is an important sense in which wrongs and failures have to be remembered. It would be irresponsible to assign a post in the church requiring dependability to somebody who had a record of being unreliable. To that extent we cannot ignore character flaws, but that is a different matter from our personal relationships in which we are to be accepting of other people despite their weaknesses and shortcomings.)

3. The practice of formal forgiveness has largely dropped out of our culture. People say "sorry" or "I apologize" when they make a mistake or cross us, and we say "it doesn't matter" or "don't mention it," but seldom are we in a position where it seems appropriate to say "I forgive you." What matters is that we should not hold other people's offenses against them but should treat them with continuing love and care.

Showing Hospitality (4:9) One particular example of brotherly love—an area where special tolerance for other people's faults is required—is hospitality.

The first Christian congregations had no church buildings of the kind

---

4:11 The verb *provides* conveys the sense of lavish provision at one's personal expense. It originally described wealthy Athenians paying the costs for supplying a chorus for the theater, just as today a corporation might sponsor a concert.

To whom belongs the glory? *To him* could refer to God or to Christ. The parallel of 5:11, the analogy of other similar statements in the New Testament, and the fact that the earlier

that are now considered essential by most Christian groups (so much so that the word "church" makes us think first of all of a building rather than of people). They met in the homes of the members or hired buildings used for other purposes. Church meetings, therefore, were impossible without willingness to entertain the church. If the center of the church meeting, or at least a frequent feature of it, was a meal, the burden of hospitality extended beyond simply providing a room, even though people will generally have brought their own provisions or contributions to the common stock with them. Moreover, Christian teachers traveled a good deal from one congregation to another, necessitating the provision of hospitality. There was no real alternative to this, since inns were either nonexistent or in general of such a kind that respectable people preferred to stay with friends.

Showing hospitality is particularly demanding, and Christians needed to be reminded to show it to one another. But the accent lies on the last phrase, *without grumbling*. The arrival of guests can be inconvenient for many good reasons, and guests themselves can be awkward people. Therefore, Christians must give hospitality without grudging and without grumbling, whether secretly or openly.

The practice of hospitality is commended in Romans 12:13 and Hebrews 13:2, and being hospitable is a quality desirable in church leaders (1 Tim 3:2; Tit 1:8). There are numerous illustrations of the practice in the New Testament (for example, Acts 16:15; Rom 16:5, 23). If the need today is less because of the existence of church buildings and hotels, we may still have to ask whether the practice was inherently helpful to the life of the church and whether the injunction in this verse needs to be fulfilled not simply because it was practically necessary in the ancient world but because it had spiritual value in its own right.

Spiritual Gifts and Their Exercise (4:10-11) Peter commands next that members should use their spiritual gifts. This stands alongside the duties to pray and to show love as the third mark of the strong church. These two verses form an amazingly compact and complete

part of the verse speaks of glorifying God all favor understanding God as the antecedent of *him*. On the other hand, the word order here (where "to whom" directly follows the name of Jesus) and the analogy of Revelation 1:11 and 1 Clement 20:11-12 and 50:7 favor a reference to Jesus. With some hesitation we opt for the latter view.

The *Amen* at the end of the statement is an acclamation that it is true. Although amen

summary of New Testament teaching on ministry. The following points are significant:

1. Although Peter wrote to churches that had groups of elders (5:1-4), the duties of the latter appear to be primarily pastoral oversight of the members. But other tasks of ministry should be carried out by any members of the congregation who have spiritual gifts. The gifts are not in any way confined to the elders or to any other group separated from the rest of the congregation. It is high time that the churches today got back to the New Testament and asked serious questions about their understanding of ordination to *the* ministry, which in practice tends to confine most forms of ministry to a limited group of ordained people. God doesn't appear to be bound by such limits in bestowing his gifts.

2. A church's ministry depends on God's distribution of spiritual gifts. The idea is that God equips the members of the church for mutual service rather than that they have natural abilities for these tasks. The word "gift," often translated as "spiritual gift," is derived from the word for "grace," and not from the word for "spirit." Thus the thought is primarily of receiving a gracious gift from God, which is to be shared and passed on to others. The person with the gift is regarded as a steward of the grace of God in its many, varied forms. Although the word "grace" primarily refers to the loving quality of God toward sinful, needy people, it can also refer to *what* he graciously gives to them or to *the way* in which grace manifests itself.

3. It follows that God's gracious gifts are to be exercised in serving. When Christians receive God's grace, it is their responsibility to share with fellow Christians. What has been given to an individual has been given for others, and that person is merely the agent of God in passing it on. Consequently, the main thrust of verse 10 is that gifts are to be used *to serve others.* The point is trite, but it perpetually needs repetition, that when a person does anything in the church, the purpose is to serve other people, to do something for their good.

It is worth observing that the concept of serving others is virtually new

is normally used as a response to what somebody else says, a writer can include it after his own statement to indicate that others should agree with him by saying it (see 5:11).

Such formulas may well have been used at the end of Christian meetings. Hence some have supposed that here we have a formula indicating the end of an epistle (with the implication that 1 Peter consists of two independent pieces joined together at this point).

in Christianity or at least strongly characteristic of it. Neither in the Old Testament nor in the Hellenistic world of the time was the concept of work as service to be found. It stems from Jesus, who lived out what he taught in Mark 10:45 and Luke 22:24-7. When Paul talks about esteeming others more highly than ourselves, part of his thought is that we are to serve others. The word "serve" is derived from serving at table and reflects the sentiment that the person who is served is greater than the person who serves (Lk 22:27). Yet Jesus was prepared to take this lesser position. This is the attitude that his followers must show—especially in the church.

4. Two gifts for service are singled out, in contrast to the fuller lists in Romans 12, 1 Corinthians 12 and Ephesians 4, but between them they cover the other forms. The first of these is *speaking*. Peter's command, however, is not to encourage people to use this gift but to prescribe how it is to be used. The speaker must speak as one who utters the words of God. An unusual Greek word is used which is generally used of divine revelations such as the words Moses received from God to transmit to the people of Israel (Acts 7:38; Rom 3:2). Christian teaching is similarly based on divine revelations (Heb 5:12). Peter's meaning, however, is not absolutely clear. Does he mean that the speaker in church is actually conveying divine revelations to the congregation or that the speaker is to behave in the same way as one who is conveying divine oracles?

Either way, what is implied for the way in which the speaker is to behave? The command may be a warning against the inclusion of the speaker's own ideas or merely human opinions as opposed to the divine words. Or it may be a reminder of the sacred character of the utterance and, therefore, of the need for a proper sense of reverence and responsibility. Or it may be more of a promise, that if God calls a person to speak, he will provide him with the right words to speak. The parallel with the next clause, which refers to the supply of divine strength for the task of ministry, strongly suggests that the thought of divine provision of what to say may well be basic here. We can conclude that if a person

But no New Testament letter actually concludes with a doxological statement; in every case we have a benediction of some kind on the readers. Therefore, regarding doxological statements as marking the ends of epistles is dubious. They simply mark breaks in the thought motivated by the subject matter.

receives a message from God, he or she is obligated to be faithful in transmitting it.

5. The second type of activity is broadly called *service,* and must refer to non-verbal activity in the church, such as the performance of charitable deeds to the needy (Mt 25:44; Acts 6:2; Rom 15:25). Peter is usually assumed to be saying that such tasks can be carried out thanks to the spiritual strength that God gives to the servant. But he might mean that the servant is to pass on to others the strength that God himself freely and generously provides.

6. The final clause indicates why there was stress on the *words of God* and *the strength God provides.* The ultimate purpose of service in the church is that, in everything, God will be glorified (compare 2:12). God should be seen at work in the speaking and in the serving so that people will praise him and not praise the speakers and the servers. (Although they will express their appreciation to them, support them financially where this is appropriate [Gal 6:6] and give them due esteem and obedience, they will see through them to the God whose servants they are.)

All this praise takes place *through Jesus Christ.* If we approach God through the one mediator as sinners seeking forgiveness, this is still true of our approach as justified sinners, praising God for his grace and presenting our prayers to him. The whole of Christian experience takes place in the name of Jesus.

Peter adds his own ascription of glory at this point. He is stating that glory belongs, as a matter of right, to Christ—and through him to God. The clause is in the indicative mood, expressive of a statement of fact, and not in the form of a wish. The force is thus that God is to be glorified through the service rendered in the church because it is to him that glory belongs and not to his servants. Glorifying God's servants detracts from God's glory—even if his servants should be regarded as standing in his place on the principle that "he who receives you receives me, and he

Notes: 4:12 There is clearly a break at the end of 4:11, marked by the doxology, and a fresh start at 4:12, marked by the address *Dear friends.* Yet the topic treated in the new section is not essentially different from what preceded it. In verses 7-11 Peter moved away from advising directly on the Christian response to persecution (1-6) to outline how the church ought to live under persecution (though, in fact, what he said would be true for the church at any time). Now he has more to say directly on persecution and feels it necessary

who receives me receives him who sent me" (Mt 10:40).

We may want to glorify God's servants as a way of glorifying God, but to do so goes clean against the sense of this passage. It surely follows that all idolizing of God's servants, for example, by using such titles as "the Lord Bishop of X" or "the Very Reverend Mr. Y" or by lionizing popular preachers, should cease to be practiced in the church. There is a serious danger arising from the development of personality cults in the church. On the other hand, showing real gratitude and affectionate love to all who serve their fellow Christians is all too often neglected.

Suffering, Joy and Judgment (4:12-19) Suffering is not easy to bear. People may have different thresholds of pain, so that one can bear a greater intensity without flinching than another, but everybody has the point where the pain is experienced as pain. There are also different kinds and degrees of pains that we experience; some can tolerate some forms more easily than others. When we experience something that is really hard to bear and that appears pointless (in contrast with the harsh sting of an antiseptic cleansing a wound), we immediately ask, Why is this happening to me? This question is a protest against the fact that we suffer while others do not and presupposes that suffering ought not to happen to anyone. Peter "answers" this question in this section of the letter. He gives a number of reasons for having a different attitude, one of joy rather than outrage. Then he goes on to warn his readers about a possible danger to be faced. Finally he stresses that suffering is an occasion for praising God and that Christians should face it with tranquility and persist in doing good.

The Strangeness of Suffering (4:12) Just as the world finds the behavior of Christians perplexing (4:4), so Christians may find the reaction of the world to them perplexing. What they experience at the hands of the world is described as a fiery experience, a painful sensation, something that they feel shouldn't happen to them.

to make a fresh start on the subject by a new address to his readers. Although he goes over some of the same ground as before, he has fresh things to say.

The fact of a break and a new beginning at 4:11/4:12 is universally recognized. The explanation for it in terms of the composition of the letter is a matter of debate:

1. I have suggested that Peter is returning to his main subject after giving some teaching not so directly related to it. We should not forget that biblical writers, like anybody else,

Right at the outset, in the way that he describes it, Peter begins to explain the character suffering builds. The "fiery experience" is the same process as is employed for the refining of metals (Prov 27:21), and already in this letter Peter has commented on the parallel between the purifying of metals in fire and the testing of Christian faith in various kinds of trials (1:7). The point is emphasized by the word *trial* (also used in 1:6). It is a moot point whether we are to understand it to mean temptations that aim at the destruction of faith or trials that intend both to strengthen it by exercising it in adverse conditions and to test its reality and quality.

Thus Peter is saying (1) that suffering under persecution should be seen as a means of testing faith and (2) that such testing is something to be expected in the Christian life and should not be regarded as strange. The rationale for such testing is spelled out more fully in 4:17, but already in 1:6-7 Peter had indicated that successful testing leads to future experiences of praise, glory and honor. The strong faith of Christ's people redounds to his glory.

The Outcome of Suffering (4:13) Peter next indicates more clearly how it is that suffering is not something strange and alien to the Christian life but rather an occasion for rejoicing. The basis for his argument is the statement that, when Christians suffer as Christians, they are participating in the sufferings of Christ. And he implicitly concludes that they will also share in his future glory when it is revealed. The practical application is that because of this they should now rejoice in their sufferings. Each of these points needs some explanation.

1. In 2 Corinthians 1:3-7 Paul comments on a severe affliction that he

---

can go off on tangents. Peter now deals with what to do in specific situations of hostility such as were no doubt being experienced from time to time in various of the congregations he was addressing.

2. It could well be that the author paused in the composition of the letter at what was a convenient point and felt that he had to make a fresh start when he returned to the task. We must remember that ancient methods of composition were different from ours. Even a short document like this letter could take a long time to produce, given the appalling quality of ancient writing materials and the practice of dictation.

3. The break has suggested to some scholars that two independent documents have been joined at this point, both dealing with persecution. Whereas the first one deals with the future prospect of persecution, the second deals with its present reality. However, attempts to find differences in style, outlook and even authorship between the two parts of the letter

had experienced. Though he never states what it was explicitly, it was most probably some form of persecution or physical ailment related to his missionary work. He notes how the members of the church at Corinth were enduring patiently "the same sufferings we suffer." This can only mean that they were suffering similar sufferings to Paul for similar reasons. Now Paul experienced the comfort of God in his sufferings, and he expresses his confidence that just as the Corinthians were sharers or partners in his sufferings, so too they would be in his comfort.

Taking this as a clue, we can say that Peter saw Christians as enduring the same kind of sufferings as Jesus and for the same reasons. They were suffering at the hands of those opposed to God and his sovereign rule, and as part of the cost of bringing salvation to the world. (Of course, the sufferings of Christ were significantly different in nature and scope. Jesus was the unique mediator between God and mankind, bearing in his body the sins of the world. Nothing in the New Testament even remotely suggests that Christians—not even the saints or the martyrs—can share in the task of atoning for sin.) Peter's thought might also mean that just as the sufferings of Christ led to righteousness—in the sense that he was tested by the things that he suffered and emerged righteous—so too the sufferings of Christians lead to righteousness. Thus there are two possible ways in which Christians may be said to share in sufferings like those of Christ.

2. Christians will be overjoyed, literally "rejoice, being filled with exultation" (see 1:6, 8), at the revelation of his glory. Peter is contrasting the humble, hidden appearance of Jesus on earth with the visible splendor of his reappearance at the End (see 1:11). This sight will fill his

---

have not found general acceptance. Possibly, Peter incorporated pre-existing materials in his letter or that he drew from more than one source.

4:13 The possibilities of interpretation of the first part of the verse are: (1) Christians imitate the sufferings of Christ (see 2:20-21); (2) Christians share mystically in the sufferings of Christ by being baptized into his death and forming part of his body; (3) Christians share in the "messianic woes," the sufferings which, in Jewish teaching, were thought to herald the coming of a new age; (4) Christians share in an experience of suffering that leads to righteousness.

The view I have adopted is that Christians suffer just as Christ suffered and, because the sufferings are of the same kind and for the same purpose, they can be said to share in his sufferings. They are caused by the opposition of evil to God, part of the general cost of bringing salvation to the world (but not of atonement, which is unique to Christ) and the way through which God brings his people to righteousness.

followers with joy. Their rejoicing will be caused by the fact that Jesus, whom they have served, will be given the honor that belongs to him.

Peter's thought also includes, at least implicitly, the fact that Christ's followers will share in his glory, just as they have shared in his sufferings. The logic of the sentence demands this, and, if there were any lingering doubt, it is dispelled by the statements in 5:1 and 5:4 and by the clear declarations of Paul in Romans 8:17 and 2 Timothy 2:11-12. (See also the comments on 1 Pet 1:11 and 2:7.) The danger always lurks that such a promise may lead to people suffering or serving for the sake of their own future glory. But the thought is there in the New Testament, and we should not shrink away from it as if it were too dangerous to handle. Peter typifies the right attitude: he can see how Christians should be so taken up with the glory of Christ that they do not think about their own glory. They see their own glory as part of the glory of Christ, and so they are prepared to suffer because it will redound to his honor.

3. Consequently, Christians should rejoice when they are called to suffer rather than regard the experience as strange and unwelcome. In other words, the way in which suffering is faced, namely as something to be rejoiced in, determines whether Christians will rejoice at the last day and share in the glory of Christ. Two false attitudes need to be noted, however.

First, Peter does not mean to rejoice in the suffering itself. There are people who take a perverse joy in suffering for various reasons (such as the sympathy it brings them or so that they can make themselves out to be pitiable creatures or because it makes other people suffer by looking after them). Such masochism is far removed from Peter's thought. He is not suggesting that Christians should want to suffer. On the contrary, he is talking about rejoicing that, when suffering does come to us, we can see it as a sharing in Christ's suffering.

Second, Peter is not urging Christians to seek suffering, even suffering for Christ. Suffering remains unpleasant and is never described as anything else. It is not God's ultimate will that we should suffer. Therefore, we should not seek it and take a perverse delight in being persecuted.

4:14 It may be that the Spirit of glory contains an allusion to the Shekinah, the manifest glory of God that filled the tabernacle in the wilderness (Ex 40:34-35). Many MSS add here, "he is blasphemed on their part but glorified on yours," which Michaels (1988:265-66)

The Blessings of Suffering (4:14) We might expect that after the promise of future joy for the persecuted there would be a more detailed statement of what this might involve, still in view of the future. But to our surprise Peter continues by talking about a present experience of joy for them. Peter paraphrases the words of Jesus: "Blessed are you when people insult you . . . because of me. Rejoice and be glad, because great is your reward in heaven" (Mt 5:11-12; compare Lk 6:22-23).

In this verse Peter refers to exposure to shame, which was a peculiarly harsh experience in a world where "losing face" was taken much more seriously than in modern Western culture. In Old Testament times those who stood by their faith in Yahweh experienced this (Ps 69:10; Heb 11:26 actually speaks of Moses bearing "disgrace for the sake of Christ"), and Jesus himself was humiliated (Rom 15:3). It is not surprising that his followers should have to suffer in the same way for their allegiance to him (Heb 13:13). To be insulted publicly is, by normal reckoning, a source of misery. But Peter echoes Jesus and says that, on the contrary, appearances are deceptive. In fact, *you are blessed.*

Here Peter repeats what he said in 3:14, but in that verse he did not explain how such people are blessed. Here he does: To be blessed is to be the object of God's favor and the recipient of his blessings. The English word "blessed" is perhaps not the best one to use, as it sounds rather old-fashioned and otherworldly. Yet it is hard to find a suitable equivalent. The GNB uses "happy," which correctly expresses the element of joy that such people should feel, but it fails to bring out the *spiritual* aspect—that this happiness is due to their favorable treatment by God. They share in the serene, untroubled life of God himself because he bestows his gifts on them.

Such happiness may arise because one actually receives God's gifts or because one has the confident expectation of receiving them in the future. In Matthew 5:3-12 the disciples are generally said to be blessed now because of what they will become and receive in the future. This is true of the promise in verses 11-12 that those who are insulted will receive a great reward in heaven (see 1 Pet 4:13). But in verses 3 and

regards as part of the original text, pointing out that blasphemy against the Spirit is not committed by Christians but by their persecutors.

10 Jesus promises "theirs *is* the kingdom of heaven," and it is wrong to insist that this merely means that in the future they will enjoy the blessings of the kingdom.

Jesus clearly taught that the kingdom was already present in his preaching and mighty works and became powerfully present in the world after his resurrection (see Mk 9:1). It seems, then, that Peter joins together the description of the persecuted in Matthew 5:11 with the promise in the preceding verse of a present experience: "Blessed are those who are persecuted because of righteousness, for theirs *is* the kingdom of heaven."

The nature of the blessing is remarkable: *the Spirit of glory and of God rests upon you.* It seems probable that Peter started to write simply "the Spirit of God" but then decided to bring in the idea of glory, and so produced a slightly awkward phrase. The belief that the Spirit of God can rest on people is found in the Old Testament with reference to the elders of Israel (Num 11:25-26) and the Messiah (Is 11:2). Therefore it is not surprising that the Spirit should rest on the people who belong to the Messiah and who share his path in life.

A Jewish statement comments that those who suffer are privileged before God, for the glory of God rests upon them. But behind Peter's statement there may also lie a recollection of the statement of Jesus that, when his followers were put on trial, the Holy Spirit would give them the words to say (Mt 10:19-20; see Acts 7:55-56). Here, however, the thought is not so much of the Spirit's help for those undergoing trial but rather of the divine favor on faithful Christians. The Spirit conveys a share in that glory which they will share fully with Christ when he appears (4:13). Already they are beginning to be glorified (see 2 Cor 3:18).

4:15 Two of the terms used here have caused puzzles. The first is *criminal.* The Greek word simply means "wrongdoer," but the NIV correctly interprets it in context as *any other kind of criminal,* though this possibly restricts the range too narrowly by using such a strong word as *criminal.* One does not need to be a criminal to incur a driving penalty. Tertullian's view that the word means "sorcerer" should be laid to rest.

The second word is in Greek *allotriepiskopos,* which most probably means "a person who meddles in other people's affairs" (as in NIV, *meddler).* Suggestions of such people being present in Christian churches are found in 2 Thessalonians 3:11 and 1 Timothy 5:13, and they are not exactly unknown today. The form of the Greek sentence suggests that, whereas the first three categories refer to actions culpable at law, this one refers to noncriminal activities. (For this criticism as being made of the Cynics, see Balch 1981:93-94.)

Suffering for the Wrong and the Right Reasons (4:15-16) A condition was built into the promise in verse 14: that of suffering *because of the name of Christ* or, in other words, suffering that is morally undeserved but arises purely out of opposition to Christ and his people. But, as Peter had already noted with special reference to slaves in 2:20, people suffer for other reasons. They may suffer, for example, legal penalties for such crimes as murder and robbery. (The crimes named are probably extreme examples, used to make the point vividly, rather than actual crimes known to have been committed by some of Peter's readers.)

No Christian is perfect either, and, even when we are disliked or attacked for being Christians, those who dislike us can usually seize some element in our conduct which is distasteful to them. Christians who feel discriminated against because of their faith may well in fact be an object of derision because of their own faults and failings: a censorious attitude toward others, a sharp temper, intolerance, petty dishonesty and so on. Peter warns his readers to beware of persecution as a consequence of un-Christian conduct. He has already made the point that there is no credit or glory in suffering for that reason, even if it is borne patiently (2:20). On the contrary, it is implied here, Christians should feel ashamed of themselves.

But no one needs to be ashamed of suffering as a Christian. Rather we should recognize that suffering because of our faith is a way of bringing glory to God. We overcome the fear of shame when we recognize that God does not see it like this. He is glorified by the faithful witness of his people.

In verse 16 we have one of the very few uses of the word "Christian"

4:16 The word *Christian* has a Latin form of ending *(Christianus)* of the type used to indicate the followers or partisans of a leader (as with *Caesarianus*). Luke tells us that it came into use at Antioch, probably within ten years of Christ's death.

Praise God that you bear that name is a doubtful paraphrase. The Gk is literally, "glorify God in this name." Kelly argues that the use of "name" here and in verse 14 reflects a Semitic idiom which means something like "on account of" (1969:186, 190-91). Therefore, the phrase means "on this account, namely that you are called upon to suffer as those who bear the name of Christians." Michaels adopts the variant text "in this matter" (1988:269-70). The simplest explanation is "Glorify God [in the way in which you behave] in respect of the name [of 'Christian']."

For the place of shame in the New Testament world see B. J. Malina (1981).

in the New Testament (see also Acts 11:26; 26:28). Its use on every occasion supports the view that it was a nickname bestowed by outsiders on followers of Christ, a term of opprobrium which gradually was taken over by Christians themselves. The term highlights a time when the members of this new religious group, known among themselves as "disciples," "believers," "holy ones" and so on, were recognized as a distinct sect by society and given a name that corresponded to one of their most conspicuous characteristics—namely, that they put Christ at the center of their faith and life. Peter's readers, dubbed with the name "Christian," will bring glory to God by suffering for it. And only suffering directly associated with opposition to Christ brings glory to God.

Suffering As a Part of Judgment (4:17-19) The thought expressed in 4:17 is not easy. Therefore, we should note first that the verse should be linked not to verse 16 but rather to the whole paragraph, especially to verse 12. There Peter described suffering as a "fiery trial." Now he develops this idea. The period of time has begun in which God is judging the world: he is "weeding out" those who are opposed to him and those whose faith in him is hypocritical (which is not the same thing as a weak but genuine faith).

Nevertheless, as in Amos 3:2, where God punishes those whom he has especially chosen as his people because of their sins against his known will, so here too God's judgment is directed against the church as the company of people who *profess* to believe in him. The church is not so much here God's *family* (NIV; Gk "house") but rather his temple (2:1-10). It ought to be holy and pure. The effect of persecution is to show up in the church those who really believe and are prepared to stand firm and those who do not really believe and so fall away when under trial. This judgment also purifies the true believers, encouraging them not to commit shameful acts.

All this shows that being a Christian is no easy option. We have to do with a God who is to be served with fear, even though he is our Father (1:17). Christians need to take the judgment of God seriously. From the grim experiences of believers, however, one can draw the conclusion that the judgment on those who actively reject the gospel and oppose

---

4:17 For the use of imagery derived from Ezekiel 9:6 and Malachi 3 see Grudem 1988:181-4 and Schutter 1989:154-66.

believers will be all the more grim. The sufferings of Christians will seem mild by comparison.

The point is reinforced by a quotation from Prov 11:31 (LXX). The righteous man is the man who stands in a right relationship to God under his covenant with Israel. He corresponds to the believer. He is saved and reaches eternal life in the next world, only by grace and not without suffering (1:6; 4:12). By contrast the godless sinner hasn't a glimmer of a chance; he will, as it were, vanish from view, for he will not be able to face the dazzling holiness of God.

How, then, should Christians react to suffering?

1. They should be sure that they are suffering *as* Christians and not because of their own wrongdoing. If so, then their sufferings are *according to God's will*, not something outside his control and purpose. One can state this point rather negatively by saying that, if the forces of evil impose suffering on Christians, then this falls within the sphere of what God allows and what he can use as part of his purpose. He can use suffering to purify and strengthen his people and to bring glory to his name.

Can we also put it positively? Are we to say that God intends his people to suffer? Hard though it may seem, the answer to this question is affirmative. It was God's will that Christ should suffer to redeem his people, and Christ was obedient to that will. To be sure, the need arose only because of the evil in the world, but in a world where evil exists its defeat is possible only through suffering.

Part of the mystery of evil is that it cannot simply be wiped out but only overcome by the suffering love of God incarnate in Christ. It would be wrong, then, to say that God's will for us is suffering for its own sake or because he delights in suffering; on the other hand, it is right to say that God's will for us is suffering because there is no other way that evil can be overcome. When we suffer, it is not a sign of God's lack of love or concern for us.

2. Those who suffer can confidently place themselves in the care of God. He is their faithful Creator, whose concern is lasting and not confined to the moment of creation. To so commit oneself to God is to

---

4:19 *Themselves* is literally "their souls," but this is simply a Semitic form of expression for the reflexive pronoun with no further significance.

follow the example of the psalmist and of Jesus (Ps 31:5; used by Jesus in Lk 23:46; compare 1 Pet 2:23).

3. Such commitment to God's care must be accompanied by doing what is good (2:12; 3:16). The reality of faith in God is evidenced by upright behavior, just as in the Old Testament "knowing God" is identified with righteous and compassionate social conduct (Jer 22:15-16; see 1 Sam 2:12; Jer 4:22; 9:24). Faith without action is not faith.

Peter's message here is strange to Christians who are tempted not to take judgment seriously. Perhaps we have been alienated by the idea of a God who is petty, ready to punish every trivial offense with severe punishment. Some people are all too ready to identify the sufferings and disasters in other people's lives as the divine penalty for evildoing.

This passage, however, is concerned not with retribution for sins committed by God's people but with the testing and strengthening of faith and the overcoming of evil's power by loyalty to God expressed in suffering. It is expressed in general terms of what may befall the church, and the idea that God sends persecution upon his people as a punishment for their sins is simply not present. Rather it affirms clearly that, right in the midst of the testing which God imposes on his people, they can prove his faithfulness to keep them by his power for their future salvation (1:5).

Leadership in the Church (5:1-5) A football team consisting of a number of enthusiastic players, each with their own particular skills, is not likely to be fully effective without some leadership to assign roles to the players, to initiate a strategy for the game, and to encourage and help them. A coach or manager has to provide leadership, and bear responsibility. The analogy with the church is apparent. A church may have any number of individuals gifted by God with spiritual gifts of teaching and service, but it will still need leaders responsible for making decisions, providing encouragement, keeping people on the right path and so on. Especially in situations of stress and conflict will this need be most urgent (see Heb 13:7, 17-18).

The leadership of a church may be one person or a group, self-appointed or democratically elected. Ideally leaders will be persons called and equipped by God for the task. But there is no way of getting anywhere without it. A group may resolve that they will act together to lead themselves—something that is practicable only for very small groups—but inevitably the members will recognize those more gifted for leadership and will accept them or try to curb their influence.

In this passage Peter assumes that there will be leaders in the church. He does not discuss how they are appointed or what their duties are. He is concerned, as so often in biblical discussions of leadership, with how they do their appointed duties. It is the style of the leadership that matters. Reading between the lines we can form some idea of what these leaders' duties were, but the main point is the way in which leadership is exercised.

The inclusion of these instructions here in a section of the letter on the church under attack indicates that they are particularly important for the persecuted church and should be interpreted primarily in that context. Nevertheless, what Peter teaches here applies generally to church leaders at any time; the instructions are timeless in their relevance.

Peter's comments on leadership in the church raises questions about his readers' relationships to their church leaders and to one another. And Peter does have something to say to the younger members of the congregation and then to everybody. His pattern of teaching again resembles that of a Household Code, a set of instructions for the different members of a family, including its servants, that outlines their duties toward one another (as in 2:11—3:12). The "household" pattern is used ecclesiastically here as the basis for harmony within the whole church.

All this raises questions of application to which we must return: Is the "system" of church leadership here one which reflects the influence of a culturally determined pattern of secular life? If the modern world has a different household code, are we free to adopt a different pattern in church life?

First, however, we must see what Peter actually says to the elders, to the young and to everybody.

The Elders (5:1-4) The Greek word translated "elder" simply means an older man (as in Acts 2:17), and sometimes it is not clear whether it means an older church member or a church leader. In ancient communities it was considered appropriate for the older men, or at least some of them, to act as the leaders. Leaders in Jewish communities were called elders, both in Old Testament and New Testament times. Thus the development of the use of *elders* to mean "leaders" was a natural one. Although the *elders* here are contrasted with the *young men,* the description of their tasks makes it clear that Peter is thinking of them in their capacity as church leaders. We can probably assume that not all the older men were active in leadership (in any case, some may have been too old to take an active part in leading the church), but the line between respect for the older men as older men and for them as church leaders would have been a fuzzy one.

Peter addresses himself to them on the basis of his own position, which is expressed in quite a remarkable way. Here is the apostle who is presented in Acts as the original leader of the church in Jerusalem— the first apostle among equals, if you like. Here is the apostle whom Paul calls the apostle to the circumcised as he himself is the apostle to the uncircumcised (and Paul doesn't let his readers forget it!). Here is the apostle who is venerated from an early date as the founder of the Christian church in Rome, or at least as its first bishop. By A.D. 96 he is venerated as a leading martyr. Whether or not this present letter is directly from the pen of Peter, one would expect the instructions to reflect his authority and leadership in the church; but not a word of it. Of course he refers to himself as an apostle in 1:1; yet thereafter he slips into the background. And when he comes to this section of the letter he is content to say that he is a fellow elder, another older man called to leadership on the same terms as they are.

Two questions arise. First, what has happened to Peter (or to the image of Peter if the letter is not from his pen)? Is it too naive to say that he has grown in humility as a result of his Christian experience? Certainly nothing could be further from the picture of a pompous bishop. We note that the picture of Paul in Acts 20:18-35, also addressed to elders, is not dissimilar. In both cases we have people who did have leading positions in the church but who knew how to act humbly in the exercise of them.

Notes: 5:1 It is noteworthy that, just as 3:13—4:6, which deals directly with facing persecution, was followed by 4:7-11, which deals with the common life of the church and the exercise of spiritual gifts, so too 4:12-19, which deals with the suffering of the church, is followed by 5:1-6, which is concerned with mutual respect and leadership in the church.

Selwyn's view that verse 1 refers to Peter's presence at the transfiguration of Jesus, seen

Second, why does Peter appeal in this way at this point in the letter? Certainly the elders were expected to heed what was said to everybody earlier in the letter, written with the authority of Peter as apostle. But at this point, when he turns directly to them, instead of taking a stand on superior authority he prefers to appeal to them as one on their level. Perhaps he is bringing them up, as it were, to his level, saying, "Your task in your local congregation is the same in essence as mine in caring for the church more widely." Thus he impresses upon them the significance and responsibility of their task in the church. He is appealing to them on the basis of the common task that they share.

Peter's appeal is further based on his position as *a* witness of Christ's sufferings. This could mean nothing more than that Peter was an eyewitness of the death of Jesus (admittedly, he may have been in hiding for part of the time), or that he was a witness to the sufferings of Jesus in the sense that he gave his testimony to them. But, while such thoughts may be present, it is more likely that the phrase refers primarily to the way in which Peter shared in the sufferings of Christ. Two things demand this interpretation: first, the parallel syntax of the next phrase, which speaks of his sharing in the future glory, suggests that the thought here is also of sharing in something; second, it is probable that the "fellow" element in "fellow elder" should be carried over to the present term, in which case an exclusive reference to Peter's eyewitness role at the death of Jesus is ruled out.

Finally, Peter appeals as *one who will share in the glory to be revealed* in the future. He puts this thought, expressed also in 4:13, even more firmly in terms of the Christian's personal sharing in the glory of Christ. Verse 4 shows that what Peter expects here is something that would be shared by his readers. In the light of this we can say that those who testify to what Christ has suffered on their behalf will share in his glory. And this surely implies that those same ones who testify to Jesus' sufferings are prepared to take a share in that suffering (as 4:13 makes clear).

Consequently, what Peter says here by way of self-description is in fact

---

as an anticipation of his future glory, is unlikely, even though 2 Peter 1:16-18 is a clear reference to that incident (1947:228-29).

5:2 The phrase *serving as overseers* is omitted by important manuscripts, but it has early attestation and is more likely to have been dropped by later scribes who did not think that it was appropriate to describe elders as fulfilling the role of bishops.

intended as an appeal to the church leaders. He is saying that they too must be prepared to testify to the sufferings of Christ and take their share in them. Then they too will receive their share in his glory.

For what is Peter appealing? Verses 2-3 contain Peter's deep concern for *how* the church leaders carry out their duties.

1. Peter exhorts a style of leadership for the elders in terms of a metaphor drawn not from the household but from the field. In the Old Testament God was pictured as the shepherd of his people, and the leaders whom he appointed as undershepherds (Ps 23:1; Is 40:11; Ezek 34). This picture was taken over by Jesus, who saw himself as the shepherd of God's flock (Mt 15:24; Lk 12:32), and he employed the analogy of his own task to that of the shepherd quite frequently. New Testament authors naturally applied the metaphor to the church's leaders (Jn 21:16; Acts 20:28-29; Eph 4:11; Jude 12) under Christ as the chief shepherd (1 Pet 2:25; Heb 13:20).

What does the picture convey? As developed in the various biblical passages, it brings out the desperate need of sheep for a shepherd: to keep them from wandering away in their stupidity; to protect them from dangers from wild animals and thieves; to feed them; to find them, even at personal risk, when they are lost; to prevent one animal from taking advantage of others; to maintain unity within the flock; and to exercise individual care. Many of these applications were made exclusively with reference to Jesus, but they apply by extension also to those who are his undershepherds in the church.

2. The fellow elders should act like *overseers*. This is the Greek word from which the word "bishop" comes, and so we might translate instead "serving as bishops." The Greek reflects a Hebrew word used, in the Dead Sea Scrolls, of a person with supervisory responsibilities. In early Christian writings it is often linked with the task of shepherding (Acts 20:28). Peter already used it in 1 Peter 2:25 to describe Jesus as the chief overseer of the people of God.

3. They are to do their task willingly. A person who is appointed as

5:3 *Those entrusted to you* translates a noun which is etymologically "your portions by lot"; however, this original sense was by now lost. The idea is rather of what is distributed to different people by God. The word most probably refers either to the individual spheres of duty of each elder within a congregation or to the individual churches addressed in Peter's letter. It is not clear whether Peter envisages only one or several elders within each cona leader must do his job not simply because he has been so appointed—and therefore halfheartedly—but from a real desire to serve. Various reasons for halfheartedness can readily be envisaged. For example, from an early date the church felt an obligation to provide financially for those whose Christian service prevented them from earning what they needed to live (1 Cor 9:7-12; Gal 6:6; 1 Tim 5:17-18; compare Mt 10:10). Such provision inevitably induced some to undertake church work, especially if they were out of work. But the danger was that people would then do so primarily because of the financial gain. A legitimate expectation of proper remuneration could turn into greed for money, and this is what Peter condemns here.

It is also possible that the leaders were in charge of the common funds of the church and that Peter has in mind the danger of misusing them for their personal benefit. Leadership should not be undertaken for what it brings to the leader—financially or otherwise—but eagerly for service to others (in the spirit of 2 Chron 17:16). Paul uses the same word "eager" to characterize the attitude with which Christians should give their money away (2 Cor 8:1-2, 19; 9:2). Thus Peter highlights two significantly different attitudes to wealth.

4. People may also undertake leadership not so much for financial gain but more for the sake of personal prestige and power. The desire to be a leader rather than one who is led is strong in many of us. Fair enough. But high is the danger of *lording it over* other people and failing to show them proper respect. This attitude, typical of worldly rulers, was condemned by Jesus (Mk 10:42), who warned his disciples not to emulate the world's ways.

Those entrusted to you implies that elders have to tell other people how to live; they may well have to exercise discipline over others. But it must not be done in a domineering manner, which is an abuse of their position. Christ modeled leadership as service to those who are led and not as the promotion of self-interest. Here Peter returns to the pastoral imagery: the elders should be examples to the flock, demonstrating in

gregation. The latter is, however, the more likely.

5:4 The picture of the crown may be drawn from festive celebrations (Is 28:1-5), royal imagery (Jer 13:18) or from games imagery. Probably ideas from all three sources would be suggested to the minds of the readers, but the games imagery ("you will receive" means "you will win") is uppermost (1 Cor 9:25; 2 Tim 4:7-8; Jas 1:12; Rev 2:10).

their conduct of leadership the same qualities they wish to see in the congregation generally. Respect must be mutual between the leaders and the rest of the congregation.

In verse 4, finally, Peter promotes the right motivation for good conduct as elders: Christ's future return. He is thinking of the Second Coming, or *parousia,* when Christ appears to reward and judge his people (Col 3:4; 1 Jn 3:2). Retaining the pastoral metaphor, he speaks of Christ as the *Chief Shepherd* (compare Heb 13:20) to whom the undershepherds are responsible. As we have seen, Christ himself also acts as a shepherd, caring for the flock (2:25). Christian leadership is thus a sharing in the leadership of Christ under his direction.

Implicitly, therefore, it is he who bestows honor on faithful servants. The metaphor shifts to that of an ancient athletic contest. The winning contestants were rewarded with a garland "crown" woven from the branches of the olive or some other tree. Peter describes the crown as being made of amaranth flowers, which did not fade away. The same contrast between perishable earthly garlands (even of amaranth) and the everlasting, imperishable divine award is made by Paul in 1 Corinthians 9:25. The crown is a metaphor for the glory that the church leaders will share with Christ.

Young People (5:5) The next instruction is addressed to young men. What about the middle-aged men, we may ask, and what about the women? Ancient ways of categorizing people by age varied somewhat, but it does appear that men were commonly divided into young and old. The dividing line came around the age of 40, although some would argue that it came at 60. Either way, a clear distinction existed between the young and the old, and leadership tended to be confined to the latter. It would appear that the women were not considered as leaders and were expected to be quiet and obedient (see 3:1-6).

Such a situation must have caused some tensions, since the church inevitably had people ministering and serving although they were still in the younger age bracket. Jesus himself was no more than 30 when he

5:5 The phrase *in the same way* is odd, since the elders have not been told to be subject to anybody. Two explanations are possible: (1) The phrase simply introduces the next item in a list (see 3:1, 7) and means something like "in the same way as the previous group have to act appropriately to their station, so too you must act appropriately to yours, and in your case this means being subject to the elders"; or (2) the point may be that, just as the elders

began his ministry, and his disciples would have been about the same age or younger. Paul and Timothy are explicitly said to have been young. We can well believe that some young people may have been restive if they found themselves excluded from a voice in the church's affairs. Peter's instructions are directed to maintaining the traditional state of affairs: the young men are instructed to submit to the elders or older men (compare 3:1, 5).

The Congregation as a Whole (5:5) That the elders and the young should have *mutual* respect is demonstrated by the final instruction in this section. All the members of the church must show humility toward one another. The Greek verb for "clothe yourselves" conjures up the picture of attaching a piece of clothing by some kind of fastener.

A long tradition of interpretation sees here a reminiscence of the scene in John 13:1-5, where Jesus put on an apron in order to wash the feet of the disciples as a vivid model of humble service. Whether a conscious allusion is present or not, the story in John undoubtedly provides forceful backing for the teaching here. Just as Jesus humbly served his disciples, so too each member of the church, whatever his station, must show humility toward each of the other members, whatever their station (see 3:8). Leadership does not mean superiority and the right to domineer. "Followership" does not confer the right to undermine.

Behind the instruction lies Peter's conviction, based on the teaching of the Old Testament (Prov 3:34) and shared by other Christian writers (Jas 4:6), that God is opposed to proud people and favors the humble. In the final analysis, the proud, who boast in their self-sufficiency and independence, feel that they have no need of God and are actually opposed to him and his gospel. Their pride is also seen in their attitude to other people, whom they regard as less important than themselves and treat with disdain.

By contrast, the humble are those who recognize that they are totally dependent on God. Out of that relationship comes the recognition that they are no better than other people. Sadly, it is possible for Christians

---

are in effect to show respect for the young by not lording it over them in the exercise of their office, so for their part the young are to show respect for the elders by accepting their instructions. These two explanations may complement each other. It is unnecessary to regard the *young men* as a special group of novitiates, preparing for an office in the church.

to conceive themselves as dependent on God ("I am the Lord's humble servant") but to act as if his favor toward them entitles them to think of themselves as better than others.

So then, we have studied Peter's advice on relationships given in the context of a patriarchal society. Does it still hold true for us today?

1. If we start from the end, the basic principle in the second part of 5:5 is appropriate in any society which recognizes that we are all made in the image of God, that we are entirely dependent on him and that we owe respect to one another, regardless of our position. This principle must surely apply in the church. Mutual respect, courtesy and service are the natural outworking of this gospel principle. Leaders are to be respected and obeyed: "hold them in the highest regard in love because of their work" (1 Thess 5:13). But leaders must also show respect to those whom they lead.

2. Peter discusses how leadership should be exercised, not how leaders are appointed or what their functions are. He simply takes for granted the system of eldership. But there are variations on the system elsewhere in the New Testament. In some churches the first converts had a leading role (1 Cor 16:15-16); in others "deacons" served alongside the elders. There may already have been a diversification of function among the elders, which led in time to the post-NT development of a local "bishop" presiding over a group of elders. No one particular setup for leadership appears to be sacrosanct.

What does matter is that leadership be exercised in the right spirit of service for others and that necessary responsibilities for the good of the congregation be carried out. Peter suggests that these responsibilities are analogous to those necessary in caring for a flock of sheep. If we wish to adopt a different picture of leadership, we must be sure that these same responsibilities are properly undertaken.

3. Different systems of leadership may thus be possible. A patriarchal setup is not necessarily appropriate for all times and places. What does not seem possible is that the church can exist without leadership. The concept of God (or Christ) as leader appears to be fundamental and cannot be done away with.

4. Leadership is for the good of the members. At times there may be a tension between the good of the members and the good of the church.

But if the church is God's church, then the interests of the members individually as the people of God and of the congregation as a whole should ultimately coincide.

Concluding Practical Advice and Encouragement (5:6-11) This section begins by taking up the wording of 5:5 and developing the point further. Intended as a conclusion to the whole section on facing up to hostility (3:13—5:11), since suffering is the real theme of the whole letter, it also forms an appropriate conclusion to the whole letter. It falls into three sections. Verses 6-7 treat the Christians' relation to God: they must maintain a humble attitude before him and put all their cares into his hands. Verses 8-9 treat Christian experience in relationship to the devil, who is to be resisted, just as he is by other Christians throughout the world. Verses 10-11 promise ultimate victory as a gift of God and ascribe glory to him for it.

The Christian life is a curious blend of trust in God and resolute action based upon it. Because of this, two opposite dangers afflict Christians. At the one extreme is the attitude that believes so wholly in the sovereign power of God that the Christian life requires no effort. We call this quietism, the view that through communion with God his power will enter our lives and change us. It can be linked with a kind of fatalism which believes that whatever happens to us is God's will and that all will turn out for the best. We do not need to worry about opposition because God will take care of us.

At the other extreme is the attitude that stresses the need for vigorous effort in the Christian life. I once read a printed sermon in which the preacher explained that Christianity was often depicted as setting forth the commandment of love and promising an injection of power to enable us to fulfill it—rather like a horse being drugged so that it may run faster in a race. The point made in the sermon was that the promise was a mirage and that Christianity was simply a moral code that we must keep. The springs of action lie in the code itself.

Both points of view are clearly extreme and, as such, false. Christians must find a balance. This is what Peter offers us in this section: the promise of divine help for those who trust in God and the command to resist the devil with all our might stand together. Nevertheless, the relationship between the two sides remains difficult. How is the divine power related to our human effort? How does God strengthen weak human wills? Doesn't the difficulty of trying to reconcile the divine and the human aspects of Christian living call in question the whole construct?

The best that we can do is to admit that the problem is irresolvable—but then so are many other problems of a philosophical character, and we live without solving them. The "quietist" way of life breaks down on the fact that we do have our own wills and cannot totally lose them in surrender to another power. The "activist" way of life is free from such philosophical problems, but it leaves us with a sense of defeat, faced as we are by an impossible ideal. Clearly Peter was not worried by the problem. He found that in experience God's power enabled Christians who trusted in him to overcome temptation and suffering.

Submission to God (5:6-7) Having instructed his readers to submit humbly to one another because God gives his grace to the humble, Peter reminds them that at the root of such mutual submission lies a basic submission to God himself. To submit to God means basically that we are conscious of our humble status as his creatures. We are prepared to do his will, whatever that may be, at the cost of curbing our own sinful and selfish desires. In the words of an Old Testament prophet, this is the basic attitude that we should have toward God: "What does the Lord require of you? To act justly and to love mercy and to walk humbly with your God" (Mic 6:8).

Peter goes on to say that such submission is *under God's mighty hand.* When this type of expression is used in the Old Testament, it generally speaks of God's power to intervene in history for the sake of his people. God's hand is his protecting power (Ex 13:9; Deut 26:8), displayed when

---

Notes: 5:6 A similar pattern of thought—submit to God but resist the devil—is found in James 4:6-10. The same verse from Proverbs is cited as in 1 Peter 5:5. This suggests that we have here a common pattern of teaching for persecuted Christians, which has been drawn on by both James and Peter. The existence of a "persecution code" behind a good deal of New Testament teaching was detected by Selwyn (1947:439-58), and, while he may have pushed his case too far, he seems to be right in basic principle. There are links also with the teaching of Jesus, suggesting that Christian teaching in this area was built up on the basis of the tradition of his sayings. Verses 10-11 have parallels in 1 Thessalonians 5:23-24; 2 Thessalonians 2:16-17; and Hebrews 13:20-21.

A saying of Jesus is reflected here, found in Matthew 23:12; Luke 14:11 and 18:14 (see

his people are oppressed and crying out for deliverance. Thus Peter is telling his readers to trust in God's power to care for them. But the same expression can also be used of the way in which God exercises discipline and imposes suffering on his people (Job 30:21), and so the thought here may rather be that Christians are to submit themselves to persecution, knowing that God's will is being carried out through it.

We can, perhaps, combine the two ideas by saying that Christians are to entrust themselves to the mighty power of God which, although it may allow them to undergo the "fiery trial," will nevertheless protect them and bring them safely through. Paul says something similar in 1 Corinthians 10:13 when he asserts that God will not let us be tempted beyond what we can bear but will also provide a way out so that we can stand up under it.

Submitting to God in this way leads to exaltation by him. The person who is content to submit to humiliation in this world, out of submission to God, will be exalted by God and will share in the glory of Christ (4:13; 5:1). This will take place *in due time*, which must mean the time of the Second Coming and glorious appearing of Christ (see 1:5; 4:7). Possibly also Peter means that before too long God will bring persecution to an end.

Although humility before God involves submission to the suffering that may be in his purpose for our lives, we can and must put all our anxiety into his hands. This is an attitude which is basic to faith in the living God (see 4:19). It is found already in Psalm 55:22 (which is echoed here), and strongly emphasized in the teaching of Jesus (Mt 6:25-34; Lk 12:22-32; see Phil 4:6). Indeed, anxiety can separate us from God because it is so often over matters of worldly concern and reflects a lack of faith in God to provide for our needs (Mk 4:19; Lk 21:34). There is

Mt 18:4). In its full form it states that those who exalt themselves will be humbled by God and vice versa. The implication is that, if you want to be exalted then, you must be prepared to be humble now. And so we have the formulation here in 1 Peter that says "humble yourselves, *so that* God may exalt you." Paradoxically, humbling oneself now for the sake of being glorified later is *not* truly humbling oneself and will not have the selfishly desired effect! It is interesting that Paul sees a different effect arising from humbling oneself: "Was it a sin for me," he writes to the Corinthian church, "to lower myself in order to elevate *you?*" (2 Cor 11:7).

5:7 *Cast* is a particularly strong expression; we are to place our worries in God's hands—and leave them there!

no need for anxiety if we trust in God because he makes us the object of his concern, as Jesus again makes clear (Mt 6:26-30; Lk 12:24-28; see 1 Cor 9:9). The Good Shepherd, unlike the hired servant, is concerned for his flock (Jn 10:13; compare Mk 4:38).

Resisting the Devil (5:8-9) The main point of the next short section is contained in its initial commands, which reflect 4:7. But these commands are motivated by a fresh perspective. So far Peter has spoken very much of persecution as a fiery trial that forms part of God's purpose for his people. Now he notes that trials can have negative outcomes.

Real testing carries the risk of failure. When a metal girder is tested to see if it is strong enough to form part of a bridge, the point of the test is to submit it to a comparable load so that, if it is going to give way, it will do so in the test and not at a later point. Testing of Christians carries the risk that they will fall, and sometimes they do fall in the face of temptation and persecution.

Of course, it is not God's will that they should fall. This desire is to be attributed to the devil, who appears here for the first and only time in the letter. His power expresses itself in the lives of those who oppose and persecute Christians, just as the power of God is active in the lives of Christians. He is characterized as the adversary of God's people. His activity is vividly described in terms of a lion who roars to frighten his prey (Amos 3:8) as he prowls around looking for somebody to eat.

Faced by this threat, Christians have a twofold responsibility. First, they must be alert to recognize what is happening in the world. Peter repeats the command to be self-controlled (1:13; 4:7), supplemented by a command to be alert. If the first command literally refers to avoiding the effects of intoxication, the second refers to casting off sleepiness and remaining wide-awake. Such actions must characterize believers as they wait for the return of Christ (Mk 13:35; 1 Thess 5:6). They must recognize the dangers that lie in wait for them so that they are not caught unawares.

5:8 *Enemy* can mean a legal adversary in court (Mt 5:25; see Rev 12:9-10, where the devil is the accuser of God's people), but here the word simply means an opponent.

The picture of the lion is found in Psalm 22:13 (see Ezek 22:25). It is applied to the situation of persecution in 2 Timothy 4:17 and Revelation 13:2. The image of the devil stalking his prey is found in Job 1:7.

Devour symbolizes total destruction: the devil's aim is to cause believers to become apostate.

The devil's tactic is to *deceive* his victims rather than merely to challenge them openly or intimidate them. Spiritual discernment is therefore vital.

Wherever the devil is active, then the second responsibility arises. Christians are to resist the devil (Eph 6:13; Jas 4:7). They are not to be passive and let themselves be eaten up. But surely a man hasn't much chance against a lion! Of course he hasn't, but Christians resist the devil by *standing firm in the faith*. They take the attitude of the Lord's Servant: "Because the Sovereign Lord helps me, I will not be disgraced. Therefore have I set my face like a flint, and I know that I will not be put to shame" (Is 50:7). What Peter is talking about is not putting strength into believing but drawing strength from what we believe. As Goppelt aptly states, "Faith overcomes evil not as a human attitude but thanks to its content. . . . That is why the exhortation about persecution in the letter does not conclude with this imperative but with the promise in verse 10" (1978:342).

But before this promise Peter gives a further word of encouragement. Those who resist the devil know that the same kind of sufferings are being experienced by their fellow believers everywhere. This does not imply that there was an imperial law forbidding Christianity (as some later church writers seem erroneously to have supposed) or any kind of organized worldwide persecution. Rather, Peter knew that the kind of local opposition to Christians in Asia could be found in many other places. Anti-Christian sentiment was spreading. Furthermore, we can also note that, if this letter was written at a time when opposition was growing in Rome itself, this example probably would have widespread effects in encouraging similar attitudes elsewhere.

The Divine Promise (5:10-11) The body of the letter concludes with this vigorous statement of the gracious power of God. Many similar statements in other New Testament letters are expressed in the form of a wish or prayer. This one is different in that it is stated as a promise;

5:9 Why does Peter mention the worldwide spread of persecution at all? Is he simply saying "You must stand firm as an encouragement to other Christians"? Or "You can take some comfort from the fact that you are not alone in what you are undergoing"? Or is he suggesting that the widespread nature of persecution indicates that it is the last "grand fling" of evil against God and that the End cannot be far distant? Perhaps he is saying that there is a fixed amount of suffering appointed for God's people and that it is being rapidly exhausted by this worldwide persecution, in which case it cannot last for ever.

it is an assertion of what God will certainly do. If there is a condition attached to it, it is that the readers will follow the commands in verses 8 and 9. This is a promise to those who resist the devil.

It begins by characterizing God in the most fundamental way as the God of all grace—the God whose grace is sufficient for every type of situation (see 2 Cor 1:3). Thus the ultimate fact about God is that his character is sheer love and concern for the welfare of his people, even in their sufferings. He has called them to be his people (1:15), and his intention is that they should share in his own eternal glory. This promise clearly indicates that this intention concerns all believers and not just church leaders (as in 5:1, 4) and that they will all share in the glory of Christ and not merely rejoice at seeing his glory revealed (4:13). This calling and its effects take place through God's action in Christ.

There is an intended contrast between the *eternal* glory that lies ahead of Christians and the *little while* during which they must suffer. Here Peter is repeating thoughts from the beginning of the letter (1:6) so that the letter is neatly rounded off by drawing together what has been said earlier. (He is also expressing a comparison made by Paul in 2 Corinthians 4:17.)

During this period of affliction God will help his people. Four verbs are used to bring out different aspects of this help: (1) God will *restore* or repair whatever is damaged, so that the believer will be fully complete to face up to whatever lies ahead (if we have been defeated in the past, this does not mean that our capacity to face future conflicts will be impaired); (2) God will make us *strong*, or stable, imparting courage and strength to weak believers; (3) God will make us *firm*; (4) God will make us *steadfast*; he will establish us so that our defenses rest on a firm foundation and will not be undermined. It may be hairsplitting to differentiate the senses of the various verbs used in this way. They are piled up rhetorically to emphasize that God will strengthen us in every way to face up to persecution.

5:10 The phrase *in Christ* (3:16; 5:14) characterizes Paul's theology. He uses it to indicate how the whole existence and experience of the believer is determined by God's saving action in the death and resurrection of Christ. Peter shares this Pauline manner of expression, which is not in the least surprising given that Peter and Paul did meet and talk to each other. Here the phrase should probably be taken with the verb *called* rather than with the noun *glory*. It is important to observe that the sentence can be taken in two ways. It could

It is appropriate to express a doxology in praise of God at the thought of his gracious promise to his people. The form of the statement indicates that it is intended as a doxology or ascription of praise and glory to God, but the content is that Peter ascribes *power* to God. This is entirely appropriate in the context. If verse 10 has indicated what God will powerfully do for his people, it is appropriate to celebrate in a doxology the fact of this power. The intention is to say: "to God belongs all or ultimate power," so that the promise in verse 10 itself rests on the Christian belief that God is not only gracious but also omnipotent. He will ultimately triumph over evil.

☐ Closing Greetings (5:12-14)

Just as there was an accepted pattern for the beginning of a letter in New Testament times, so too there was a customary way of concluding, once the body of the letter was complete. Christian writers followed the general pattern but gave it a fresh Christian character. Naturally this included greetings to the writer's friends and also from other persons associated with him. A mention of anybody who had particularly helped in writing and transmitting the letter was usual; indeed, a letter often functioned as a commendation for the person carrying it. A Christian form of blessing would replace the usual secular "farewell" (surprisingly found at the end of the Christian letter in Acts 15:29) or other closing greeting.

These features are found here at the close of this letter and confirm that it is a personal letter from Peter to people whom he knows.

The Writer's Helper (5:12) Peter explains that he has written his letter *with the help of Silas.* Silas is generally held to be the same person as the companion who accompanied Paul on his missionary work after his separation from Barnabas (Acts 15:40) and who figures in the opening greetings of 1 and 2 Thessalonians. He may have been the bearer of this letter (see his role along with others in Acts 15:22), in which case the commendation of him as a faithful brother would be appropriate for

---

mean that *after* we have suffered a little, the God who has called us to future eternal glory will strengthen us. It can also mean that the God who has called us, who have suffered a little, to future eternal glory, will strengthen us during our sufferings. It is better to take *suffered a little while* as a contrast to *eternal glory* (that is, to adopt the second alternative).

5:11 For the use of a doxology at the end of the body of a letter see Romans 15:33 (see note on 1 Peter 4:11).

congregations who did not know him.

Nevertheless, it seems strange that a missionary of such standing as Silas should require such a commendation. Moreover, to say in effect *I have sent to you briefly* sounds odd. Consequently, many scholars think that Peter means that Silas also acted as the scribe who wrote the letter. But, whereas it is probable that a person like Tertius, the scribe of Romans (16:22), was merely the scribe, possibly Silas had a larger share in the composition of this letter.

Silas is described as a *faithful brother*—"faithful" in the sense of trust-worthy rather than believing. This description makes sense if Peter has entrusted the composition of the letter to him and indicates that Peter is confident in his ability to represent his thoughts faithfully.

To say that the letter is *brief* is somewhat conventional. In fact apostolic letters were considerably longer than ordinary secular letters. But if by this time people knew about the length of Paul's letters, then a new standard of comparison had been established. Romans and 1 Corinthians are each four times the length of 1 Peter.

The real point of the sentence, however, lies in the summary statement that concludes it: The letter is one of encouragement and instruction. We need both of these words to bring out the meaning of the Greek word often translated "exhort" (see 2:11). The letter is in fact largely couched in the imperative mood, encouraging the readers to believe in the promises of God and to act on them. The letter is also a testimony, in which Peter speaks out of his own personal experience as a Christian. He has testified that *this is the true grace of God.* "This" must refer to the total experience described in the letter, and the readers should stand fast in this testimony. Right to the end Peter continues to encourage them.

Notes: 5:12 *Whom I regard* is a strong, positive statement, not an ambiguous one. It need not imply that other people doubted Silas's trustworthiness.

For the view that *I have written* refers to the actual writing (as apparently in NIV), see Goppelt (1978:347-9).

The clause *stand fast in it* is in fact a relative clause in Greek, which makes the imperative form somewhat strange. Moreover, why does Peter need to say that this is the *genuine* grace of God? Were there people who thought that their experiences of suffering meant that they were not in the gracious hands of God? Peter encourages them to believe that precisely in the midst of sufferings they are experiencing grace. A reference to heretics who claimed that the readers were excluded from divine grace is unlikely, since nowhere in the letter is there any hint of heresy as a problem affecting the readers.

Peter's Colleagues (5:13) It was customary to add greetings from those who were with the author at the time. *She who is in Babylon* must be the church in Rome. The affectation of personifying a congregation as a female figure was facilitated by the fact that "church" is a feminine noun in Greek and by the tradition that saw Israel as a female figure, the bride of God. *Babylon* is a pseudonym for Rome. The nickname expresses the fact that here Christians felt themselves to be in exile in a foreign land, a city of luxury and sin, the oppressor of God's people. Its use is derived from the way in which Babylon figured in the Old Testament as the oppressor of God's people. The Jews applied the nickname to Rome after the destruction of Jerusalem in A.D. 70, but long before this date Roman writers themselves had begun to characterize their own city as another Babylon in view of its luxury and increasing decadence.

Also associated with the greetings is *Mark*. This must be a reference to John Mark, who went with Paul on his first missionary campaign though he made a premature exit for reasons unknown. Despite Paul's unwillingness to have him as a colleague on his subsequent campaigns, the two came together again (see Philem 24; Col 4:10; 2 Tim 4:11). Peter's description of him as *my son* probably means that Peter was responsible for bringing John Mark to faith in Christ (as Paul brought Timothy; 1 Cor 4:17) rather than that he was simply his senior colleague.

The link between the two men at this later stage in Peter's career is entirely plausible. We do not know why Mark is specially mentioned here in a letter to Asia. Since we know nothing of Mark's career subsequent to his missionary work with Barnabas in Cyprus (Acts 15:39), we certainly cannot rule out missionary work in Asia. But perhaps, because Mark was increasingly the colleague of Peter, as the tradition preserved

---

5:13 The feminine form *she* has sometimes been taken to refer to Peter's wife, and this view has been supported by the reference to Peter's son in the next part of the verse. But Mark is almost certainly John Mark, who was Peter's son only in a metaphorical sense. For the personification of the church as a woman, see 2 John 1, 13.

Some have argued that the Christian use of *Babylon* as a sobriquet for Rome is derived from the Jewish usage, which does not date from before A.D. 70, so that this letter must also be given a late date. But the Christian use is surely related to the persecution of Christians by Nero at an earlier date. It is likely that Nero was making threatening gestures even before Rome's Great Fire and the execution of Peter and Paul (see Thiede 1986:154, 173-84; 1987:221-9).

by Papias indicates, Peter would naturally associate his closest colleague with him in the conclusion of his letter.

Tokens of Affection (5:14) A greeting is an indication of affection and interest in the readers. It is an expression of friendship and love between people who are separated from one another. Therefore it is natural for Christians to express their feelings in this way.

The new element in the situation is the command to the readers to greet one another with a *kiss of love.* The kiss was a greeting sign of brotherly affection used by the Jews and practiced also among the disciples of Jesus. (The traitorous kiss of Judas was unusual not in that Judas kissed Jesus but rather in that he turned an accepted sign of affection into a means of betrayal.) The kiss was not associated with erotic desire.

It is not clear whether Peter asks the readers to exchange kisses as a sign of the affection between himself and them or in order to encourage affection among themselves (see 1:22). Could it be that as the readers heard the letter read and responded by kissing one another, they felt that the absent writer was himself included in the fellowship and the ties binding them to him were strengthened?

The practice of kissing has been revived in some modern Christian groups. There may be situations where it is awkward, even embarrassing or misleading, if the kiss is not an accepted way of showing affection between people of opposite sexes—or of the same sex, if it has wrong (for example, homosexual) associations.

Here is a good example of where the cultural significance of a particular action must be taken into account. If, for whatever reason, kissing is inappropriate, some other culturally acceptable substitute should surely be adopted in its place. The danger is to do nothing, keeping other Christians at arm's length. In the Christian fellowship there ought to be a greater degree of mutual love and care, especially for single and lonely people, than in society and large, and the church may well need to take the lead in showing love to such people and in confirming and conveying it to them by suitable symbolic actions.

The Benediction (5:14) Peter concludes by wishing *peace* to his

---

5:14 The kiss is elsewhere called a "holy kiss" (Rom 16:16; 1 Cor 16:20; 2 Cor 13:12; 1 Thess 5:26). Only here is it called a *kiss of love*—that is, of Christian love. For a full discussion, see Stählin (1974).

readers. The Pauline practice was to conclude a letter with a "grace" benediction that echoed the secular greeting more closely, but Paul also wishes his readers peace (Rom 15:33; compare 2 Cor 13:11; Eph 6:23; 1 Thess 5:23). If grace is the source of divine blessings, peace sums up the content of the blessings. The old Jewish greeting is filled with new meaning when it is said and received in the light of what God has done in Christ. Like love, peace is one of those Christian words that has been sadly devalued by its loose, secular usage. Somehow we need to recover its original force.

Peter appropriately addresses his greeting to the people who are *in Christ*. Peter shares Paul's basic description of a Christian as a person whose existence is determined by the crucified and risen Lord. And the exclusivity of the description should not be ignored: Outside of a relationship with Jesus Christ as Savior and Lord there is no real, lasting peace.

Bibliography

Andersen, F. I.

1986   "Yahweh, the Kind and Sensitive God." *God Who Is
                Rich in Mercy: Essays Presented to Dr. D. B. Knox.*
                Edited by P. T. O'Brien and D. B. Peterson. Grand
                Rapids, Mich.: Baker, pp. 41-88.

Balch, D. L.

1981   *Let Wives Be Submissive: The Domestic Code in 1
                Peter.* Missoula, Mont.: Scholars Press.

Bartchy, S. S.

1973   *MALLON CHRESAI: First-Century Slavery and the
                Interpretation of 1 Cor. 7:21.* Missoula, Mont.:
                Scholars Press.

Bauckham, R.

1988   "James, 1 and 2 Peter, Jude." *It Is Written: Scripture
                Citing Scripture.* Edited by D. A. Carson and H. G. M.
                Williamson. Cambridge: Cambridge University Press,
                pp. 303-17.

Beare, F. W.

1970   *The First Epistle of Peter.* Oxford: Blackwell.

Bénétreau, S.
1984   *La Première épître de Pierre.* Commentaire
               évangélique de la Bible. Vaux-sur-Seine: Edifac.

Best, E.
1969   "I Peter II 4-10—a reconsideration." *Novum
               Testamentum.* 11:270-93.
1971   *1 Peter.* New Century Bible. London: Oliphants;
               Grand Rapids: Eerdmans.

Brox, N.
1979   *Der erste Petrusbrief.* Evangelisch-Katholischer
               Kommentar zum Neuen Testament. Zürich: Benziger/
               Neukirchen: Neukirchener.

Clowney, E. P.
1988   *The Message of 1 Peter.* The Bible Speaks Today.
               Leicester, England, and Downers Grove, Ill: Inter-
               Varsity Press.

Cranfield, C. E. B.
1968   *I and II Peter and Jude.* Torch. London: SCM
               Press.

Dalton, W. J.
1965   *Christ's Proclamation to the Spirits: A Study of 1 Peter
               3:18—4:6.* Analecta Biblica 23. Rome: Pontifical
               Biblical Institute.

Denney, J.
1951   *The Death of Christ.* London: Tyndale Press.

Elliott, J. H.
1966   *The Elect and the Holy: An Exegetical Examination of
               I Peter 2:4-10 and the Phrase βασίλειον ἱεράτευμα.*
               Leiden: Brill.

1981   *A Home for the Homeless: A Sociological Exegesis of
               1 Peter, Its Situation and Strategy.* Philadelphia:
               Fortress.

Feinberg, J. S.
1986   "1 Peter 3:18-20, Ancient Mythology and the
               Intermediate State." *Westminster Theological Journal*
               48:303-36.

France, R. T.
1977   "Exegesis in Practice: Two Samples." *New Testament Interpretation.* Edited by I. H. Marshall. Exeter: Paternoster; Grand Rapids, Mich.: Eerdmans, pp. 252-81.

Frederick, S., C.
1975   "The Theme of Obedience in the First Epistle of Peter." Ph.D. diss., Duke University (Ann Arbor: University Microfilms, 1978).

Goppelt, L.
1978   *Der erste Petrusbrief.* Kritisch-exegetischer Kommentar über das Neue Testament. Göttingen: Vandenhoeck und Ruprecht.
1982   *Theology of the New Testament.* 2 vols. Grand Rapids: Eerdmans. 2:161-78.

Green, G. L.
1980   "Theology and Ethics in 1 Peter." Ph.D. diss., Aberdeen University.

Grudem, W. A.
1988   *The First Epistle of Peter.* Tyndale New Testament Commentaries. Leicester, England: Inter-Varsity Press; Grand Rapids, Mich.: Eerdmans.

Haubeck, W.
1985   *Loskauf durch Christus: Herkunft, Gestalt und Bedeutung des paulinischen Loskaufmotivs.* Giessen/Basel: Brunnen/Witten: Bundes-Verlag.

Hunter, A. M.
1957   *The First Epistle of Peter.* Interpreter's Bible. Vol. 12. New York: Abingdon.

Judge, E. A.
1980   "Slave, Slavery." *Illustrated Bible Dictionary.* Leicester, England: Inter-Varsity Press; Wheaton, Ill.: Tyndale. 3:1464-66.

Kee, H. C.
1973   *The Origins of Christianity: Sources and Documents.* New York: Prentice-Hall.

Kelly, J. N. D.

1969   *A Commentary on the Epistles of Peter and of Jude.*
Black's New Testament Commentaries. London: A. &
C. Black. Harper's New Testament Commentaries.
Peabody, Mass.: Hendrickson.

Maier, G.

1985   "Jesustradition im 1. Petrusbrief?" *The Jesus Tradition
Outside the Gospels.* Edited by D. Wenham. Gospel
Perspectives. Vol. 5. Sheffield: JSOT Press, pp. 85-128.

Malina, B. J.

1981   *The New Testament World: Insights from Cultural
Anthropology.* Atlanta: John Knox.

Martin, R. P.

1986   "Peter, First Epistle of." *International Standard Bible
Encyclopedia.* Grand Rapids, Mich.: Eerdmans. 3:807-15.

Michaels, J. R.

1988   *1 Peter.* Word Biblical Commentary. Waco, Tex.: Word
Books.

Millauer, H.

1976   *Leiden als Gnade: Eine traditionsgeschichtliche
Untersuchung zur Leidenstheologie des ersten
Petrusbriefes.* Europäische Hochschulschriften. Vol.
23:56. Bern: H. Lang; Frankfurt/Mainz: P. Lang.

Neugebauer, F.

1979   "Zur Deutung und Bedeutung des I. Petrusbriefes."
New Testament Studies 26:61-86. (Reprinted in
Thiede 1987:109-44.)

Perrot, C.

1980   *Études sur la première lettre de Pierre.* Lectio Divina
102. Paris: Cerf.

Reicke, B.

1946   *The Disobedient Spirits and Christian Baptism: A
Study of 1 Pet. III.19 and Its Context.* København:
Munksgaard.

1964   *The Epistles of James, Peter and Jude.* Anchor Bible.
New York: Doubleday.

Robinson, J. A. T.
1976   *Redating the New Testament.* London: SCM Press;
               Philadelphia: Westminster.
Salom, A. P.
1963   "The Imperatival Use of the Participle in the New
               Testament." *Australian Biblical Review* 11:41-49.
Schelkle, K. H.
1970   *Die Petrusbriefe. Der Judasbrief.* Herders
               theologischer Kommentar zum Neuen Testament.
               Freiburg: Herder.
Schrenk, G.
1967   "πατήρ κτλ." *Theological Dictionary of the New
               Testament.* 10 vols. Edited by G. Kittel and G. Friedrich.
               Grand Rapids, Mich.: Eerdmans, 5:995-96, 1010-11.
Schutter, W. L.
1989   *Hermeneutic and Composition in I Peter.* Wissen-
               schaftliche Untersuchungen zum Neuen Testament.
               2:30. Tübingen: J. C. B. Mohr (Paul Siebeck).
Selwyn, E. G.
1947   *The First Epistle of St. Peter.* 2d ed. London:
               Macmillan.
Spicq, C.
1966   *Les Epîtres de Saint Pierre.* Sources Bibliques. Paris:
               Gabalda.
Stählin, G.
1974   "φιλέω κτλ." *Theological Dictionary of the New Testa-
               ment.* 10 vols. Edited by G. Kittel and G. Friedrich.
               Grand Rapids, Mich.: Eerdmans, 9:118-27, 138-46.
Stibbs, A. M., and
A. F. Walls
1959   *The First Epistle General of Peter.* Tyndale New
               Testament Commentaries. London: Tyndale Press;
               Grand Rapids, Mich.: Eerdmans.
Thiede, C. P.
1986   *Simon Peter: From Galilee to Rome.* Exeter:
               Paternoster.

1987   "Babylon der andere Ort: Anmerkungen zu 1 Petr
               5,13 und Apg 12,17." *Biblica* 67:532-38. Cited from
               the reprint in *Das Petrusbild in der neueren
               Forschung.* Edited by C. P. Thiede. Wuppertal:
               Brockhaus, pp. 221-29.

Turner, N.

1976   *A Grammar of New Testament Greek (by James Hope
               Moulton).* Vol. IV, Style. Edinburgh: T. & T. Clark.

Windisch, H.

1951   *Die katholischen Briefe.* Handbuch zum Neuen
               Testament. Tübingen: J. C. B. Mohr (Paul Siebeck).